Burcham Harding

Brotherhood

Nature's Law

Burcham Harding

Brotherhood
Nature's Law

ISBN/EAN: 9783743351172

Manufactured in Europe, USA, Canada, Australia, Japa

Cover: Foto ©ninafisch / pixelio.de

Manufactured and distributed by brebook publishing software (www.brebook.com)

Burcham Harding

Brotherhood

BROTHERHOOD

NATURE'S LAW

BY

BURCHAM HARDING

NEW YORK
BURCHAM HARDING
144 MADISON AVENUE
1897

PRICE 20 CENTS

TO THE READER.

Copies of this book, in quantities, will be supplied on specially moderate terms to facilitate its use in colleges, schools and similar institutions, and for general distribution.

The publisher invites coöperation in giving this book as wide a circulation as possible, in the belief that human happiness depends upon a clear understanding of the laws underlying Brotherhood, or right conduct. Correspondence and suggestions to this end are solicited.

B.H.

Copyright, 1897, by Burcham Harding. All rights reserved, including those of translation. This book is copyrighted in foreign countries in accordance with the provisions of their laws and of the International Copyright Law.

PREFACE.

The aim of the writer of this treatise has been to present simply and clearly the basis of right conduct, demonstrating that it is embedded in the heart of nature.

The moral law is as firmly fixed as the heavens and the earth, and cannot change. Until mankind recognizes this fact and moulds its actions in accordance therewith, suffering and strife will continue.

It matters not whether violations of the law arise from ignorance or wilfulness; nature will demand retribution. Let all, therefore, understand the law, and teach it to others, for thus will there spring up happier conditions in the world.

It is becoming more generally recognized that moral depravity is the embodiment and outcome of man's mental states; for iniquity may abound, but if it does not enter our minds, we are unaffected by it. To remove vicious conditions from human society, requires that each person be purified mentally. A sound philosophy based upon nature's laws is the first necessity to attain this mental and moral purification.

The subject of this treatise precludes the possibility of originality; and such is not claimed. The twelve lessons are an elaboration and extension of the "Lotus Circle Manual No. I," to the authors of which the writer is greatly indebted, and also to other friends for valuable suggestions and assistance.

The chapters deal consecutively with the different aspects of the subject, carrying the reader onwards step by step. The questions at the end of each chapter are intended to facilitate class work.   B. H.

New York, Nov. 1, 1897.

TABLE OF CONTENTS

		PAGE
PREFACE		3
CHAPTER I.	The One Life	5
CHAPTER II.	One Life in All	14
CHAPTER III.	Growth	22
CHAPTER IV.	Cyclic Manifestation	30
CHAPTER V.	The Law of Action	39
CHAPTER VI.	Reincarnation	48
CHAPTER VII.	Progress	57
CHAPTER VIII.	Duality	66
CHAPTER IX.	Sevenfold Manifestation	76
CHAPTER X.	The Connecting Ray	85
CHAPTER XI.	Universal Brotherhood	93
CHAPTER XII.	The Basis of Morals	101

CHAPTER I.

THE ONE LIFE.

> "Let us build altars to the Blessed Unity which holds nature and souls in perfect solution, and compels every atom to serve an universal end"—*Emerson.*
>
> "In him who knows that all spiritual beings are the same in kind with the Supreme Spirit, what room can there be for delusion of mind, and what room for sorrow, when he reflects on the identity of spirit."—*Yajur Veda.*

The One Life pervades all regions of space and all forms. It is everywhere, boundless, infinite, eternal, the origin of everything visible and invisible, of all that has been, is and ever shall be.

The One Life is the great force and energy of nature, planning and carrying into execution. It is architect, workman and material, the great moulder of the universe and its heart.

The One Life is divided into many "lives," parts of itself. In other words, the one great force or energy of nature is sub-divided into innumerable smaller forces, or centres of force, each being inseparable from the One Life and identical in essence with it. There is no difference, save in degree, between the "lives" that are found in the minerals, in plants and trees, in animal and human bodies, for all are parts of the One Life. In one aspect, the division into "lives" is illustrated by the ocean which is divisible into drops, each of which is a part of and identical in nature with the whole; or by electricity generated in a single current, but which is sub-divided in its application, and used for many purposes and in various places.

The One Life, eternal and indestructible, may be termed the Soul of the universe. Similarly each of the "lives" is an indestructible soul, a separate and distinct centre of energy, pursuing its own course of evolution and accumulating in itself the experience gained on its onward march. Every point in space is filled with "lives," souls, or centres of force and energy, planning and moulding visible and invisible nature.

We see neither the One Life nor the "lives," but we perceive something of what they do, and the garments they put on for a time and then discard. The mineral, vegetable, animal and human kingdoms, are terms used to classify some of the forms assumed temporarily by the One Life. Light, heat, magnetism, electricity, gases and vapors, are other expressions of the One Life. The various objects around us are aggregations of "lives'" drawn together by mutual attraction, which have put on a clothing of matter. These forms endure for a certain time and then disintegrate; the "lives" throwing off their bonds of matter are then free to seek other embodiment.

The One Life corresponds to the manifested Deity, superior to which, is the Unmanifested Cause of all. Each of the "lives" is thus a part of the Deity, God-like and spiritual, carrying on its evolution in an orderly manner, directed by divine wisdom.

This unseen One Life is ever-active; from it all material and immaterial things proceed. As said above, it combines the offices of architect, workman and material. A seed grows into a plant because the One Life works within and through it, fashioning the various parts according to the plan within the seed, attracting such "lives" as are adapted to each part, and clothing them with material particles.

The One Life pervades everything in nature, its operations are universally evident. A scientist speaks of it as the law of the conservation of energy, which regulates the changes and transmutations of force, but does not admit of annihilation. Metals and rocks exhibit it in the force of cohesion binding together their particles; also, by the use of a microscope is revealed the regular formation of the crystalline structures guided by the "lives."

Magnetization of a steel bar causes the extremities to assume positive and negative polarities. If the bar be cut into any number of pieces, each will have a positive and negative end, showing that the change produced by magnetization has occurred in the "lives," which have been polarized. Chemical affinity, and combinations of gases in fixed proportions, recorded by chemical formulæ, display the operations of the One Life. The conversion of ice into water, steam, and vapor, at certain temperatures, is an exhibition of an intelligent force always at work.

In the vegetable kingdom the One Life directs growth, causing seeds to expard and attract "lives" in water, air, sunshine and soil, producing the perfect plant. Conscious intelligence is displayed, by roots striking out towards water and suitable soil; leaves and shoots, as in cellars, turning towards the light, and reaching out to grasp supports. Each seed reproduces its own kind, according to the plan or pattern contained within itself, again displaying a conscious guidance. In the animal kingdom the One Life is seen in the automatic actions of the bodily organs, heart, lungs, brain, stomach, etc. Each organ is an aggregation of "lives" embodied in cells whose past experience has fitted them to carry on the special function of that organ. Upon injury occurring to any part of the body, the "lives" exhibit conscious intelligence in hastening to its repair.

The invariable regularity of the laws governing the forces of nature contained in and ordained by the One Life, induces people to build steam and electric engines, to sow their crops, erect edifices and do all the thousand and one things of everyday life.

Every object demonstrates the existence within itself of an unseen intelligence, guiding, building and controlling it. It is important to distinguish in the mind between the outer forms of nature and the One Life which animates and builds them up. The visible stone and metal are distinct from the invisible life which binds together the molecules. The plant or tree is distinct from the life which causes its growth. The animal body with its organs is distinct from the life within. Similarly, we are not our bodies, but something within, which inhabits and uses the body, In the waking state the body is the instrument we use for carrying on operations in this world, but in sleep we remove the consciousness from the brain, and the body rests until we re-awaken. The functions of breathing, digestion, circulation, etc., are sustained during sleep by the "lives" embodied in the cells of the organs, and not by the guidance of our brain. The phenomenon of dreams shows that during sleep we possess consciousness, although it is not centred in this body, for with eyes shut and in a dark room the most vivid pictures may present themselves. Under the hypnotic influence the bodies of individuals may be used to do many things which in a normal state would be refrained from; again proving that the body and the power guiding it are separate and distinct.

The One Life is the all pervading supreme force of nature operating in everything, great and small, regulating the movements of the heavenly spheres, as well as guiding each blade of grass; drawing up water from the ocean, holding it in suspension, as clouds, and returning it as rain to nourish the earth. "Jack Frost" is but one of the familiar names we give to one of the operations of the One Life. He forms fairy pictures on the windows on a cold night from the moisture in the air of the room. The artist and his material are unseen, but the morning shows us his picture.

A close analogy can be traced between the "First Cause" of science and the "One Life," as also between the molecules of science and the "lives." Every scientist, whether his bias be towards a material or a spiritual basis of philosophy, postulates a "First Cause." He will also admit a sub-division of the universe into molecules.

Much light will be thrown upon his philosophy by considering the "One Life" as the "First Cause" in the manifested universe, beyond which is the "Unknowable" in the unmanifested. Further, let him consider the molecule, not as a mere metaphysical nonentity, but as a centre of force with a well defined purpose and history. The energy of the "One Life" working through the "lives" causes them to leave their spiritual state and gradually descend into material forms and after a period leave them again. The molecules forming the universe are both spiritual and material, spiritual in their essence as forces, but material in their temporary, outer clothing. The "First Cause" when viewed from the higher aspect is spiritual, but when looked at from below, and seen as clothed in matter, seems to us to be material.

All forms are aggregations of "lives," each of the latter being a distinct soul gaining experience and storing it. Upon the destruction of any object in nature the "lives" are liberated to return to a spiritual state, but repass from this into other material objects for further progress.

Evolution is carried on by the "lives" passing through all conditions in outer nature and accumulating in themselves the experience gained thereby. As all "lives" are parts of the One Life, it may be asked why some are found in the mineral, and others in the vegetable and animal kingdoms; why some "lives" carry on the functions of the heart, and others those of the stomach, lungs and liver? This is regulated by laws, known as Karma and Reincarnation which will be treated in later lessons.

Stated shortly, each of the "lives" is a separate soul following an orderly evolution. The forms they assume are determined by their own prior experiences; each being attracted to the conditions best suited for its further progress, in accordance with the experience previously acquired.

The manifested world exists that the countless "lives" may have the opportunity for progress. They pass from the physically formless state into contact with earth forces and then assume the material forms of nature. Originating from the One Life, the "lives" descend into matter, struggling through and connecting themselves with every condition of life and being. At the bottom of the valley of matter they identify themselves with Humanity.

In order to ascend upwards and homewards, the "God" in each person has by individual merit and effort to reach the final goal. It is the martyrdom of self-conscious existence, the crucifixion of the impulses of the body, the learning the lesson of the One Life.

"All are parts of one harmonious whole
Whose body nature is, and God the Soul."
—*Pope.*

QUESTIONS ON CHAPTER I.

1. Describe the One Life; give its attributes.
2. How do you picture Life in nature?
3. How is the One Life subdivided?
4. Illustrate this subdivision.
5. What are the "lives"?
6. Name the kingdoms of outer nature.
7. Explain in what way the "lives" are similar and dissimilar.
8. What is a soul?
9. What is the purpose of souls?
10. Are the "lives" visible?
11. What do we see as regards the "lives"?
12. How long do outer forms endure?
13. Describe how the One Life corresponds with God.
14. What relation do the "lives" bear to God?
15. Give evidence of the existence of the One Life in mineral, vegetable and animal kingdoms.
16. Does man rely upon the regular operations of the One Life?
17. What are the two aspects of every object?
18. Trace the two aspects in each kingdom.
19. What proofs are there of the two aspects in man?
20. What is "Jack Frost"?
21. What is the sphere of operations of the One Life?
22. Does science afford any analogy with the One Life and "lives"?
23. Are molecules both spiritual and physical?
24. How are natural forms composed?

25. What office have the "lives" in evolution?

26. What happens to the "lives" when a form is broken up?

27. Why do the "lives" assume varied forms?

28. What determines the form assumed?

29. For what purpose does the world exist?

30. What is the final goal of the "lives"?

31. How do the "lives" reach their final goal?

32. Explain the Unity of the One Life, and its division into "lives."

"Even though myself unborn, of changeless essence, and the lord of all existence, yet in presiding over nature—which is mine—I am born but through my own *maya*, (illusion) the mystic power of self-ideation, the eternal thought in the eternal mind. I produce myself among creatures, O son of Bharata, whenever there is a decline of virtue and an insurrection of vice and injustice in the world; and thus I incarnate from age to age for the preservation of the just, the destruction of the wicked, and the establishment of righteousness Whoever, O Arjuna, knoweth my divine birth and actions to be even so doth not upon quitting his mortal frame enter into another, for he entereth into me. Many who were free from craving, fear, and anger, filled with my spirit, and who depended upon me, having been purified by the ascetic fire of knowledge, have entered into my being."—*Bhagavad Gita*.

CHAPTER II.

ONE LIFE IN ALL.

"Souls cannot die. They leave a former home,
And in new bodies dwell, and from them roam.
Nothing can perish, all things change below,
For spirits through all forms may come and go."
—*Ovid (translated by Dryden).*

"Then the lord of all creatures said to those assembled, together: "You are all greatest and not greatest. You are all possessed of one another's qualities. All are greatest in their own spheres, and all support one another There is but one, and I only am that, but accumulated in numerous forms."—*Anugita.*

The One Life in all is divided into many "lives," similar in essence, but which clothe themselves in different forms for many purposes. The "lives" inhabiting the rock, gold, daisy, oak, spider, horse and man are similar, for all are derived from the One force or energy. There is One Life in all. This may be illustrated by water, which is found under many disguises, such as ice, liquid, vapor and steam, all separable into gases. Each of these serves several purposes; ice for preservation and purification; water for allaying thirst, cooking and cleansing; vapor for the distribution of rain and the shade of clouds; steam for a motive power in thousands of factories and vessels; gases, hydrogen and oxygen in combinations have many uses. All these are the states and components of the one element water, under various conditions and fulfilling many purposes. Similarly the "lives" although identical in essence, assume many forms, and bring about varied results.

The unity of all "lives" is seen in their mutual helpfulness and dependence, and in their adaptation one to another.

Mutual helpfulness, the basis of the law of brotherhood, is taught throughout nature. For a seed to grow, the help of all the elements is required; the "lives" in water to moisten it, the "lives" in sunshine to warm it, the "lives" in air to give carbonic acid gas, and the "lives" in the soil their mineral constituents. These "lives" as shown in the last lesson are forces or energies, progressing along their own lines of experience. Unless the "lives" in all the elements combined to help, growth would not take place, for the plant would die if deprived of water, soil, air or sunshine. This shows how entirely each is dependent upon all, and how the "lives" work together for the general benefit, as could only be done, by all being parts of the One Life.

Everything in nature, after being built up by the mutual help of the "lives," renders help in turn to something else. Mineral "lives" produce plants and vegetation, which, in turn, serve as food for animals and men. Animals are useful to man not only as food, but in lessening his toil and adding to his happiness. Nature in every division is a living portrayal of the spirit of helpfulness, or the law of Brotherhood.

Insects need the honey hidden in the deepest recesses of flowers, and in obtaining it, carry pollen from plant to plant, thus giving necessary aid in the formation of seeds. Insects help the plants and the plants aid the insects. Animals and men in breathing, deprive the air of life-giving oxygen, exhaling carbonic acid gas; trees and plants take up the carbonic acid gas, and build it into their tissues, restoring oxygen to the air which is thus purified for inhalation. Invisible " lives " are everywhere actively engaged in their beneficent offices, for all are parts of One Life.

It is a law that whenever help is given, an equivalent is received, and the same law applies to injuries, for nature is exact in rendering compensation. A philosopher would define this law as " action and re-action are equal and opposite." To make clearer the application of this law to our subject, let us analyze vegetable growth. A plant draws nourishment from the soil and water, also from air and sunshine, each of these elements being sacrificed to aid the growing plant. How do the elements receive their compensation?

The earth, air, sunshine and water absorbed by the plant lose their outer forms; soil and water are changed into sap, air and sunshine are disintegrated to build the tissues. Compensation is received in that the " lives " animating these elements are liberated from minerals and raised to the vegetable kingdom. It must be remembered that the advance is as great from the mineral to vegetable, as from vegetable to animal, and animal to man. This is nature's method of reward, to sacrifice outer forms by breaking them up, that the " lives " animating them may be liberated and raised into higher conditions, and thus gain a temporary experience in more advanced kingdoms.

Minerals are disintegrated to aid vegetation, and the "lives" enter plant forms. Vegetable life is used by animals and the "lives" are carried upwards. Both plants and animals, when used as food by man, enter human beings. In each case, by the sacrifice of the form the "lives" are advanced to higher kingdoms. The lion eats the lamb, the strong animals prey upon the weak, and it may be enquired how the helpfulness of nature is exemplified thereby?

Putting aside sentimentality, we see the outer body of the lamb sacrificed by being destroyed to feed the lion. The lamb as an entity, and the "lives" in its body are thus liberated to seek other conditions and gain further experience. That which seems to be cruelty in nature, is but her method of carrying on evolution. Sooner or later, every outward form is disintegrated; if it were not so, the world would be crystallized, the "lives" imprisoned in their present bodies, and all progress virtually cease.

This is the understanding of the purpose of those laws known as "natural selection," and "the survival of the fittest." From a lack of comprehension of nature, her ways have been deemed cruel, immoral and unjust, but with a knowledge of her methods, all is seen to be rightly and justly ordered. Some have even gone so far as to deny that nature is the handiwork of God, and attributed its operations to a devil or Satan!

The foregoing teaches a fundamental lesson in human brotherhood. All help rendered brings its due compensation. "With whatsoever measure ye mete, it shall be measured to you again" said Jesus; but the return for charitable deeds must be looked for on the spiritual and not on the material plane. If our motive in helping a needy brother is to receive back an equivalent in money or service, such is not a purely brotherly transaction, but a matter of barter or business. Brotherly actions or real charity consist in voluntarily sacrificing some benefit, comfort or possession of the personality, without asking or expecting any return from the recipient. Actions such as these last, according to nature's laws, must bring spiritual advancement. By voluntary sacrifice of personal desires we liberate "lives" in our lower nature, and raise them to a spiritual state. By following the impulses of the soul, or God within, its power for action and the spiritual will are strengthened within us. At the same time sacrifice of lower desires weakens their hold upon us. This is the crucifixion of the impulses of the body, the lesson of the One Life in all.

In the mineral, vegetable and animal kingdoms, progress is by natural impulse, the forces inherent in the One Life impel an advance. In the human kingdom, each individual must voluntarily choose to progress by his own "self-induced and self-devised efforts." Man has the option of practicing selfishness or brotherhood; of rejecting the lesson of the One Life, or of following it; but to progress he must spontaneously choose the latter, as human advance and happiness are only attainable by the practice of mutual helpfulness, the law of the One Life. In all kingdoms, not only is the help of every part necessary to the well being of all, but the failure of any to serve, is the direct cause of suffering. While all parts of a plant perform their functions, a strong, vigorous growth results; but let any part withhold its help, for instance, let the roots cease supplying sap, and the plant withers and dies. Again, while the various organs of the human body operate perfectly, there is health, strength and vigor, but let one organ, say the heart, fail to act, and death occurs. In a lesser degree, suffering arises whenever bodily action is impaired.

Throughout nature mutual helpfulness is essential for growth and progress, and wherever it is absent there arises suffering or death. The same law holds good with humanity; the practice of brotherhood would bring peace, happiness and contentment, whereas selfishness, which is the only sin, causes strife and misery. Humanity is like a vast machine; if all the wheels, cogs, cranks and parts are in perfect order, it works smoothly, but disarrangement of any part, throws the whole out of gear. Of the individuals composing humanity, each has a duty to perform for the general welfare; failure to fulfil this duty brings suffering and trouble upon all mankind.

The One Life in all, teaches the fundamental

unity of the "lives" and of all beings, and their mutual dependence and the necessity for practicing helpfulness. Lower forms are impelled to sacrifice themselves to help others which require their aid, and they thus gain progress. Human beings are equally a part of the One Life, and are inseparably bound together, but must learn of their own free will and accord to be brotherly and unselfish. We shall return again and again to this world of suffering, until selfishness be eradicated from our natures, and we learn the lesson of the One Life in All, and our unity with all mankind, in that they are our very self.

The One Life is the great heart of nature. By removing the clouds of selfishness, each can identify himself with it and beat in unison with the whole, and be a powerful factor in disseminating the beneficent influence of The One Life.

QUESTIONS ON CHAPTER II.

1. Explain how the "lives" are similar and yet dissimilar.
2. How does water illustrate this seeming paradox?
3. In what manner does Nature teach the law of brotherhood?
4. Illustrate by a growing seed.
5. When the plant is grown, does it still illustrate the law of brotherhood?
6. Is the law of brotherhood practiced in all kingdoms?
7. Does justice rule in Nature?
8. Give a statement of the law.

9. How would a philosopher describe this law?
10. Show how a growing plant illustrates this law of compensation.
11. What is compensated in the plant?
12. Describe Nature's method of compensation.
13. If an animal eats another, is there compensation?
14. Is death certain?
15. What is death?
16. How is death advantageous?
17. Why has Nature been termed cruel and unjust?
18. Is Nature the work of God?
19. What should be our motive in helping others?
20. What is real charity?
21. What is not charity?
22. How does voluntary sacrifice bring us compensation?
23. What in man is helped by right action?
24. What is the difference between the method of progress in the lower, and the human kingdoms?
25. What is the cause of suffering?
26. Illustrate by plant, and human body.
27. How can contentment and happiness be secured?
28. What is the great lesson of the One Life and the "lives"?
29. How is progress gained?
30. What binds together all mankind?
31. How can we become identified with the heart of Nature?

CHAPTER III.

GROWTH.

> "In the beginning was the Word, and the Word was with God, and the Word was God.
> "And the Word was made flesh, and dwelt among us."—*St. John's Gospel.*
>
> "Sow kindly acts and thou shalt reap their fruition. Inaction in a deed of mercy becomes an action in a deadly sin.
> "Help Nature and work on with her: and Nature will regard thee as one of her creators and make obeisance."—*Voice of the Silence.*

Growth is from within outwards. This is so because the One Life, the cause, is within. The "lives" are impelled by the force within themselves to seek a material expression, which takes place by means of growth from the invisible to the visible. The "lives" clothe themselves in that form of matter for which they have affinity, reproducing the pattern of their previous garment, expanding and modeling themselves upon it and building matter into it.

The seed shrivels up and appears to die, but the impress within of the One Life survives. It is this which bears the ideal type of the whole plant or tree, and reproduces another at the time of growth. The One Life contains the ideal types or patterns of everything in the universe.

The laws of growth are fixed and certain. An acorn produces an oak, and seeds develop plants each after its own kind; there is no confusion in nature. A knowledge of the action of the "lives" explains this regularity, for each of these centres of activity is proceeding with its evolution according to fixed law. Growth is from within, the invisible "lives" assume visible shapes; the finer substance clothes itself in grosser matter; the more rapid vibrations of the inner forces become slower as they expand outwards.

We cannot see the One Life or the "lives," but their results are visible; and similarly the finer substance and more rapid vibrations are invisible, but we know they must be present. This may be illustrated by a wheel rapidly revolving, whose spokes are then invisible, but when it turns more slowly we see them. The spokes were present even when unseen.

Again, the bass notes of a piano are loud and deep, but the sounds grow higher and lighter as the treble is reached. The wires of the treble being shorter than those of the bass, the vibrations are more rapid. Were the treble extended two or three octaves, a point would be reached where the vibrations would be so intense that no sound would be perceptible to us. The rapid vibrations produce sounds, although they are inaudible to our outer ears.

As a further illustration, a ray of light may be resolved into the seven colors of the prismatic scale. At either end of these seven colors are other scales of colors, invisible to the physical eye, but their presence recognized by the effects on chemical substances.

The ancients recognized the reality of invisible states and forces, for they spoke of God as the

Container of the Universe, who at times breathed forth, bringing all things into existence, and then inbreathed them into Himself. They also said "As above, so below"; "as in heaven so on earth"; and "there is nothing new under the sun." The ideals of everything are in the unseen, and take material forms in this world periodically in accordance with universal cyclic law, under whose guidance all things continually revolve from the invisible to the visible and back to the invisible. Could growth be watched, we should see the cell, the centre of life, divide into two cells, and these subdivide until the bud bursts the outer coat of the seed, sending roots down into the earth, and a shoot upwards to the air, building on cell to cell by subdivision. Following the method shown in the last lesson, each growing plant attracts the help of such "lives" as are necessary to its progress, utilizing all the elements and their forces.

The ancients chose the Lotus, the beautiful pond lily which blossoms on the surface of the water, with its large buds expanding from within without, as a favorite symbol of the universe. Its seed contains a miniature model of the future plant, which was taken as representing the hidden ideal type of the universe preceding its outward form. This characteristic of the Lotus caused it to be accepted as a symbol of man in the universe, explaining the saying, "Man, know thyself"; for each human being contains the type of all that exists and he should look within for Wisdom.

The Lotus plant also symbolizes the three planes of man's being. The roots in the mud represent this material world in which our bodies live. The stalks passing upwards through the water, represent the astral plane, whose forms are invisible to the physical eye, but whose influence is felt through the senses and thoughts. The blossoms in air and sunlight represent the spiritual plane where the ideal types exist, and upon which man reaches his highest possibilities. To realize his noblest aspirations, man, like the Lotus, must surmount the mud, pass through the water and reach the sunlight.

As growth is from within, so does thought precede action. First comes the idea in the architect's brain, then the plan is drawn and eventually the edifice is erected. A sculptor first fashions in his own mind the form he would portray in marble. The true artist conceives mentally the ideal he wishes to depict on canvas. The potter who would fashion in clay a vase or living thing, first thinks of that form and then moulds the clay with his hands. Thus in every case, the idea precedes its outer expression, and all growth, even in the mental world, is from within. The idea of the Universe, and all the beings it contains, is first in the thought of the One Life, but this thought has a mighty power that moves and shapes the invisible substance of Life into forms which become visible.

Ages ago it was taught that the elements contained forces within themselves, which directed, guided and moulded the outer matter. They considered these forces as possessed of intelligence in differing degrees, and personified them as sentient beings. There were several hosts of these forces, each having its special mission to direct the progression of a certain part of nature on its onward advance. This old teaching has had a further rendering in the belief in spirits in the elements, the Salamanders in fire, the Undines in water, the Gnomes in earth and the Sylphs in air. We trace the same ideas reproduced in the universal folklore and tales about sprites, fairies and other unseen forms. Mythology is full of them. The foundation for these beliefs is found in the "lives" which are the hosts of sentient beings, guiding and controlling, building up, and destroying to rebuild, the many forms of nature.

Force is unseen; only its results appear. Equally the "lives" are invisible, but they are the real agents bringing about growth and changes in all directions.

Materialism has obscured belief in everything but the physical world, but our forefathers were wiser, knowing that the unseen causes of material things must be sought and could be found. They recognized the unity of all nature in its ultimate essence.

The "lives" pass by growth and decay through everything in the world, gathering experience and storing it in their eternal essence,— through all mineral forms to the vegetable, thence to animal and man. As the result of evolution through the lower kingdoms, man's body contains the types of all that is in this world, since it passed through every vegetable and animal experience before it assumed human shape. All the "lives" are now or will become men, either in this cycle of manifestation or in a future one. Progress is by growth ever onwards and upwards, from the lowest conditions to man, the apex of evolution in this world.

In the lower kingdoms, the "lives" are controlled by general forces common to whole species. Vegetation displays a universal tendency to growth. Animals are guided by instinct and desire, which are common to them. When the human kingdom is reached, the separate individuality of each entity is accentuated, and the man within feels "I am myself and no one else."

The results of actions are stored as thoughts, which will reappear and give rise to further actions. Injuries to others impart thoughts of anger or revenge; helpful acts leave loving memories. By the law of compensation these thoughts will reappear, working from within, outwards, inciting to acts of hatred or love. "Blessings like curses come home to roost."

Growth teaches the importance of checking evil thoughts, not allowing them to stay in the mind, for they will become seeds for wrongful deeds. If evil thoughts are harbored, we are always in danger, in spite of conventional restraints.

"As a man thinketh, so is he," is true. Merely pretending to be good, but inwardly nursing angry, revengeful, and lustful tendencies, is but hypocrisy. Purification must begin by a strict watch upon the thoughts, for growth is from within.

Actions are but the reflections in matter of our thoughts. Our office is to purify the mind by eliminating all thoughts not in accord with the spirit of helpfulness, the great lesson of the One Life.

QUESTIONS ON CHAPTER III.

1. What causes growth?
2. How does growth take place?
3. Describe the action of the One Life in producing growth.
4. Why does an acorn produce an oak?
5. What are ideal types?
6. Where are they stored?
7. Do all "lives" contain ideal types? Give reasons.
8. Why cannot we see the One Life, or the "lives"?
9. Illustrate by spokes of wheel, music, and colors, why some things are invisible to us.
10. How do invisible things become visible?
11. How did the ancients describe God?
12. Describe cell growth and that of the plant.
13. What is a Lotus?
14. What two aspects of man does the Lotus symbolize?
15. How does it represent man's relation to the universe?
16. Describe its correspondence with man's triple nature.
17. What precedes action? Illustrate.

18. Does Nature prove that the inner precedes the outer?

19. How do we know the ancients were not materialists?

20. What is the foundation of folklore and fairy tales?

21. Trace the history of the "lives" in their evolution through Nature.

22. What is the apex of evolution for the "lives" in this world?

23. From an evolutionary standpoint, what does the human body contain?

24. Are the forces similar which act in the lower kingdoms, and in the human?

25. How are results of actions preserved?

26. What results are caused by injuries to others?

27. What results do helpful actions occasion?

28. When do these results appear?

29. Can the re-adjustment be avoided?

30. What lesson does growth afford?

31. Why is it useless to pretend to be good?

32. What thoughts must be eliminated?

33. What is our best moral guide?

CHAPTER IV.

CYCLIC MANIFESTATION.

> As to you, Life, I reckon you are the leavings of many deaths.
> No doubt I have died myself ten thousand times before."—*Walt Whitman.*

> "Our deeds still travel with us from afar, And what we have been, makes us what we are."
> —*George Eliot.*

> "We sleep, but the loom of life never stops, and the pattern which was weaving when the sun went down is weaving when it comes up tomorrow."—*Beecher.*

Growth is from within, proceeding outwards, and the activities of the One Life are perceived in a continued repetition of changes from an invisible to a visible state, followed by a return to the invisible. The energy in the "lives" causes them periodically to seek embodiment in objects of nature, bringing about a series of appearances and disappearances. This takes place in regular cycles, and is one of the most important natural laws.

A cycle means a ring or turning or wheel. The "lives" leaving their condition of latent activity on the invisible plane, gradually produce outer forms which having been preserved for longer or shorter periods, break up and disappear. In this way the "lives" may be said to travel in a ring or cycle, descending from the invisible along one side of the ring until they reach manifestation in matter, and returning upward by the other, to their latent state,—the descent and ascent being one cycle. These revolutions are continually repeated.

A cycle is not a circle which runs back into itself, but may be compared to a screw thread in the form of a spiral, which beginning at the lower level turns on itself in its upward course.

All the "lives" in the mineral, vegetable, animal and human kingdoms are subject to cyclic law. This is seen in the continual changes occurring in the forms of nature : everything is subject to decay ; the rocks wear away, metals corrode, animal bodies are ever changing their particles. Scientists tell us "that matter is indestructible," but this cannot refer to the outer garments, which are subject to constant decay, and infers the existence of an inner force or energy, indestructible in essence. This inner indestructible element passes through cycles of manifestation by clothing itself in temporary coverings of matter. In the mineral kingdom this can be illustrated by dissolving crystals of salt or soda, which will rebecome crystals when the water is evaporated. In the vegetable kingdom each seed has its cycle of growth, and when this is completed, it returns to its seed form. Insects have their cycles, from the egg to the larva and the winged fly, returning to the egg form. Animals have their normal life cycles, and so have human beings, for they put on a body, live in it for a period and then discard it, but the indestructible element in man lives on, and passes through lives in many bodies, as does everything in nature. Each recurring embodiment or manifestation adds something to the experience of the "lives," and on the principle of the spiral, takes them a step higher.

Cycles govern also in the world of the senses and of the desires and thoughts, for impressions of whatever kind will return in regular order. Nations and races are alike subject to cyclic law, for they return again and again with their old associates, customs and civilization; hence it is said that "history repeats itself."

Each "life" has its own special duration for embodiment, but passes through many intermediate shorter cycles. A man's span of life may be seventy years, but that will cover several cycles, such as day and night, winter and summer, prosperity and adversity, sorrow and happiness, work and recreation, which will be found to recur with great regularity. Our whole life is more or less one of routine.

When this globe took form, the substance composing it attained a certain and definite rate of vibration which will hold through all variations in any part of it, until its hour for dissolution comes. The duration of a cycle is determined by the initial rate of vibration imparted to its substance. The solar system and the globe we are now on will come to an end when the force (One Life) behind the whole mass of seen and unseen matter, has reached its limit of duration under cyclic law. "Man himself, considered as a spiritual being, is the force which determines the length of the cycle of this world. When he has finished using the globe, he leaves it, taking with him the force holding all together."

Not only the globe but everything upon it is subject to cyclic manifestation. Everywhere is seen alternation of activity and rest, as in the day and night, summer and winter, sleeping and waking, action and reaction. Small cycles make up greater ones, and these are parts of still longer ones. Thus days and nights make weeks, weeks make months, months make years and years make centuries.

Cyclic action is apparent in the ebb and flow of tides; in the currents of the ocean and the air; in the descent of rain and its return to clouds; in the blood pulsed forth from the heart and its return; in the flow of sap from roots to the leaves, and its return, and in the regular movements of heavenly bodies.

Cyclic manifestation or a series of appearances is the method used by the One Life to express itself. Man and nature have the day for activity and the night for rest. "Work while it is yet day, for the night cometh in which no man can work." The One Life causes the "lives" to assume an active existence in forms to help other "lives," and by this method nature supplies all wants and lavishly provides for man's comfort. Evolution is possible because of this wise provision of nature. "Lives" enter certain objects, remain for a period, and then the object disintegrates, liberating the "lives" to seek other experience.

Modern science has touched upon this law of cyclic manifestation, but has not yet recognized its universal character. Every atom or molecule, like one of the "lives," is a soul, eternal in its nature, passing through all forms, and storing in itself the results gained. An atom, molecule or "life," contains and is the representative of its own past history, and must acquire experience in every condition of each kingdom before advance to a higher one be permanently made.

Man is a more highly evolved and advanced atom or "life," subject to cyclic law and is undergoing experience in human conditions, having already completed it in lower kingdoms. Cyclic manifestation applied to man is known as reincarnation or rebirth, for the human soul enters a body, gains a certain experience therein, throws off the body and during a period of rest consolidates the life's work, and then returns to rebirth in another body in this world, and must reincarnate until wisdom is acquired by the practice of the lesson of the One Life.

Reincarnation is cyclic law in operation, for it is a return to life in this world, bringing with us our old differences of character and temperament, which make us all dissimilar and give each a force peculiar to himself. This cyclic return gives an explanation of life problems and the divergences in character and surroundings, which can be accounted for in no other manner.

Acts and thoughts create impressions which are reproduced when the right conditions are provided. This applies to national idiosyncrasies which reappear among people in the mass, and also affect individuals.

Every experience leaves an impression; our present conditions are but the result of past acts and thoughts, and equally does our conduct now, leave tendencies which will mould the future.

W. Q. Judge illustrated the law of impressions by saying: "Look at an electric light, and you will find it makes an image on the retina, and when you shut your eye, this bright filament of light made by a carbon in an incandescent lamp will be seen by you in your eye. If you keep your eye closed and watch intently, you will see the image come back a certain number of counts, it will stay a certain number of counts, it will go away in the same length of time and return, always changing in some respect, but always the image of the filament, until at last the time comes when it disappears apparently because other impressions have rubbed it out or covered it over."

As there is a cyclic return of impressions on the retina, so there are returns of impressions on our moral character, for, having done a thing once, there is a mental effect left which gives a tendency to its repetition. In this way habits are formed.

We are subject to periodical returns of impressions caused by anger, despondency and the like. When these arise, a strong effort should be made to create in the mind an opposite feeling of love or joy; then when the cyclic period recurs, the old feeling will return linked with the new, which will help to counteract the power of the former, and will be an excellent method of removing undesirable tendencies. As thought precedes action, our efforts to effect a change must be applied to the mind wherein the old impressions are stored.

A knowledge of this cyclic law gives a potent reason for right conduct, as the effect of each wrongful act returns in its cycle, and each individual must return to this world in his cycle, to answer for all the deeds done in the body. This knowledge is a strong incentive for ethical conduct, as it accentuates personal responsibility.

Cyclic manifestation affects the "lives" everywhere, and they by their united work cement everything in one vast brotherhood. All peoples, nations and races, as well as the "lives" in the seen and unseen worlds, are included. Each "life" is mounting from lower forms and is learning to mould, fashion and impress the matter with which it is clothed, so that it may be improved for the use of those younger brothers who are still less advanced in evolution.

There is no dead matter anywhere. Every atom in a stone contains a "life," unintelligent, formless, perhaps, judged from our standpoint, but at some period in the far distant future to be released and raised to a higher state.

The "lives" or souls ever retain the experience they have acquired, and although records, books and buildings may disappear, as souls return to this world they bring with them the memories of the past and reproduce them. Each individual indelibly impresses the record upon his own soul, and upon the return of his cycle,

CYCLIC MANIFESTATION. 37

assists in carrying civilization to a higher point. It is by cyclic manifestation, or the periodical return of the "lives" to this world, that everything is being attuned to the harmony of the choir of the One Life, wherein all are joined in Nature's great Song of Helpfulness.

QUESTIONS ON CHAPTER IV.

1. How are the operations of the One Life perceived?
2. What is the result of the action of the "lives"?
3. Is there regularity in the activity of the "lives"?
4. What is a cycle?
5. How does a cycle illustrate progress?
6. Are all "lives" subject to cyclic law?
7. Illustrate this in Nature.
8. How does science corroborate cyclic law?
9. Show how cyclic manifestation is found in each kingdom.
10. How is cyclic law perceived in the realm of the senses and thoughts?
11. Describe how there are cycles within cycles.
12. What determines the end of the world?
13. Give illustrations of cycles in our experience.
14. What is the purpose of cyclic manifestation?
15. How does evolution proceed?
16. Is a molecule similar to a soul or "life"?
17. How can man be said to correspond with a molecule or "life"?

18. What name is given to man's cyclic manifestations?

19. Describe reincarnation.

20. How does reincarnation explain differing conditions at birth?

21. Why do acts and thoughts return to us?

22. Is chance responsible for our present conditions?

23. Whence arise our characters and tendencies?

24. How are habits formed?

25. When impressions of anger and despondency arise, what should be done?

26. Why should the remedy be applied to the mind?

27. How does a knowledge of cyclic law affect right conduct?

28. How does it bear upon the practice of brotherhood?

29. Why is there no dead matter?

30. How does cyclic law affect progress?

CHAPTER V.

THE LAW OF ACTION.

"Men must reap the things they sow,
Force from force must ever flow."—*Shelley.*

"The soul contains the event that shall befall it."—*Emerson.*

"Nature is that world of substance whose laws are laws of cause and effect, and whose events transpire, in orderly succession, under those laws."
—*Bushnell.*

The law of action is the same on all planes, material, intellectual and spiritual. Every action is the result of a previous cause, which itself proceeded from one anterior. A scientific statement of this law is "action and reaction are equal and opposite." Something happens as the result of every act; however small it may be, some effect is produced, and this again causes something else to be changed. The operation of this law is invariable and it pursues its course without regard to puny man's wishes or prayers for its suspension.

In the East this law of action is called "*Karma.*" It includes both the cause and its effect, for they are inseparable except as to time. Every cause has an effect sooner or later, and every effect necessitates a previous cause. Karma is the law of action. To understand it we must bear in mind:

(a) The One Life, the universal force or energy of nature, independent of matter;

(b) The "Lives," the individual intelligences that animate the various forms of nature.

Before the rebirth of a world, the One Life exists homogeneous and undivided, one Being. At birth, when a new cycle of activity commences, the One Life divides into the "Lives" and begins its work in this world through that subdivision. This work is Karma, and is directed by the law of action. Spirit is separated from matter, but retains the link of Karma.

The "lives" emanated from the One Life, emanate in their turn new centres of energy which begin operating from within without, and multiply other minor centres. Everything, from the microbe, blade of grass, crystal, crocodile and elephant to man, is in its physical formation the product of the evolutionary forces of nature through a numberless series of transformations. The past of each thing is connected with its present, and the future will be similarly connected with the present and past. This continuity repeats itself before our eyes in all the conceivable stages of progress. It is seen in plants growing from seeds, and in the history of nations. Karma, an effect-producing cause, or a cause engendering an effect, guides and controls the "lives" in their transformations through nature. Karma is the immutable law joining the One Life to the "lives," spirit to matter, for if divorced, chaos would result.

Karma results in pain so long as the smallest atom in the infinite world of harmony is perturbed and readjustment has not taken place.

THE LAW OF ACTION.

The eternal and immutable decree of Karma is absolute harmony in the world of matter as in that of spirit. Cyclic manifestation, controlled by the law of action, prevails, until this harmonious blending of spirit and matter is attained, until mankind practises the lesson of mutual helpfulness, and follows the law of the One Life.

Applied to human relations, Karma is at the root of the ethical code; explaining rewards and punishment, and that justice underlies moral and material conditions. Harmful deeds to others bring us suffering, and kindly actions reap their compensation. This is a law of rigid justice which each experiences in operation. Karma is not fatalism, for our present conditions were fixed by ourselves in the past, and now we have free will to build the future.

Actions work in two ways; inwardly in ourselves, and outwardly as affecting others. An angry impulse, if uncontrolled, leads us to harm another, and accumulates new Karma for ourselves, leaving a seed for its return. A kindly deed also tends to repetition. What we do once is repeated more easily, and finally may become a habit and recur automatically. The effect of following evil habits becomes apparent in the weakening and destruction of the body. Bad mental habits, such as laziness, inattention, harboring thoughts of anger, fear and desire, reduce the mind to a condition of comparative uselessness, beyond control by its possessor.

Weakened bodies and minds are not only poor instruments for their owners, but by physical heredity they may be handed down by parents who give to their offspring bodies with like tendencies, as seen in cases of scrofula, consumption, cancer, as well as in hereditary tendencies to drunkenness, vice, insanity and lack of mental powers.

The outward effect of our actions upon others is easily traced, for we always act in company with our fellows. They are changed by what we do, and they again affect others. Thus the circle continually widens, and in this manner we help to change every one in the world. A pebble thrown into the water causes ripples which move every drop in that pond, and they then rebound from the margin to meet again. Good and evil deeds affect all around us, and by the law of cyclic manifestation will return to us again.

The law of action operates in each part of man's being, bringing separate results, physical, mental and moral on each plane, in accordance with his previous activities. "The parable of the talents" illustrates this. Health and strength will be renewed to us from life to life, if we use them aright, in accordance with the lesson of unselfishness taught by the One Life. The same applies to mental and moral gifts as well as to wealth and material things. Wrongful use, or devoting these talents to selfish purposes, results in our being deprived of them in future lives. Talents are retained by right use and taken away if applied selfishly.

The separate operations of Karma on the different planes of being explains diversified environments. We see some rich people with suffering bodies and morose dispositions ; others, poor but healthy and contented ; and giant intellects crippled by environments: these mixed conditions are due to the law of action operating with perfect justice on each plane of man's being.

Jesus taught this natural law of Karma as the basis of his moral code, and without it His teachings cannot be understood. In Matt.: VII, 1, 2, we read : "Judge not that ye be not judged. For with what judgment ye judge, ye shall be judged, and with what measure ye mete it shall be measured to you again" ; and in verse 12 : " Therefore all things whatsoever ye would that man should do to you, do ye even so to them for *this is the law* and the prophets," and verse 18 : " A good tree cannot bring forth evil fruit, neither can a corrupt tree bring forth good fruit." In Chap. XII, v. 36 : " But I say unto you that every idle word that men shall speak, they shall give account thereof in the day of judgment."

These quotations from the sayings of Jesus show that His philosophy was based upon a great natural law of cause and effect, that we shall receive the exact measure we mete to others ; that the law stipulates that we must first do unto others that which we wish them to do to us ; that every good action brings good fruit, and *vice versa ;* and lastly, that we are responsible for every idle word.

The beautiful teachings of Jesus will remain

idle words until this great law which underlies them is grasped.

The One Life unites humanity inseparably together as parts of one Great Self, or one individual, from which bond there is no escape. As cyclic law governs in all kingdoms, we return to this world again and again by reincarnation until the lesson of the One Life, that all parts must coöperate for the general welfare, has been learned. Each soul possesses its own past experience and seeks embodiment in accord therewith. The actions of one life determine the conditions and environments of future ones, and the law of Karma makes it apparent that as all are connected in action now, so were they in the past, and will be for succeeding lives. Death of the body does not sever connections with others, for in the immortal One Life there is no separateness. Sometimes we are injured by comparative strangers and think the wrong undeserved; but if we rely upon Karma, we know that nothing can happen unless it has been merited, even if the cause may not be apparent to us. We must have injured others in some prior life, memories of which are unknown to this brain. Karma supersedes chance and accident in the vocabulary, and secures all things to the dominion of law and justice.

An understanding of Karma explains that saying of Jesus, "love your enemies." A person cannot be our enemy without cause; and the reason we have enemies is because of injuries done to them in the past, whether in this life or a prior one. By the biblical law, "An eye for an eye," one whom we have injured must retaliate upon us, for "not one jot or one tittle shall pass from the law until all be fulfilled." Jesus admonished his followers "to love their enemies," and "this love should be the fulfilment of the law"; meaning thereby, that instead of waiting for our enemies to retaliate upon us, that we should "love them," or help them, and thus compensate voluntarily for the past injury and avoid the necessity for any retaliation.

By following this admonition of Jesus we should be brought into harmony with the spirit of helpfulness of the One Life, as well as be enabled to avoid injuries which might seriously retard our evolution.

Buddha taught the same doctrine in saying "hatred ceaseth not by hate, but hatred ceaseth by love."

How quickly the conscience reproves, when a wrong is returned by kindness. Shame and repentance are felt, and a desire arises to reciprocate with kindness, proving that the impulses of helpfulness are within us all, however hidden. Paul described the Mosaic law (Karma), as the "Schoolmaster," which brings us to the law of love (Christ).

The law of action is the law guiding evolution. The past and present mould the future. Present actions of men will create future conditions of the world. Even when this world shall have passed away, some other will be born and its life will depend upon the life results of this one.

The law of action is universal. It is seen in the qualities of all natural objects inherited from their parents. Plants may disappear leaving only seeds,—as this world may do in the future; but the qualities and forms will be invisibly stored in the seeds to guide the growth of their offspring. What is known as creation is but the re-appearance according to cyclic law of an entity which is the result of former life and action. Good and evil return. "Whatsoever a man soweth that shall he also reap."

The law of action impresses the great responsibility we have to our fellows for every act and thought, for all are united in the One Life. Evil and suffering will cease when we refrain from infringing the law of the One Life, and recognize that the heart of all nature beats in us.

QUESTIONS ON CHAPTER V.

1. Define the law of action.
2. Where does it operate?
3. Can the law of action be set aside by prayer?
4. How is this law termed in the East?
5. What is the first constituent of Karma?
6. What is the second constituent of Karma?
7. What exists before the world is reborn?
8. Describe the beginning of a cycle of activity.
9. What directs the activity, and whence comes it?
10. Describe what joins Spirit to matter.
11. How does evolution proceed?
12. Without Karma what would result?

THE LAW OF ACTION.

13. What causes pain and suffering in the world?
14. Can we escape from Karma?
15. Why are some born rich and others poor?
16. Is Karma fatalism? Give reasons.
17. How do our actions affect ourselves and others?
18. Trace effect of an angry impulse, uncurbed and curbed.
19. How are habits formed?
20. Trace effect of bad habits on mind and body.
21. What determines that a child shall inherit a weak body or mind?
22. Illustrate how our actions affect others.
23. On what planes of man's being does Karma operate?
24. Why do you find both good and bad conditions in the same person?
25. How did Jesus teach Karma?
26. Describe how Reincarnation, in conjunction with the law of action, operates upon humanity.
27. Why does death fail to relieve us of the result of actions?
28. What is the meaning of chance or accident?
29. Explain the meaning of Jesus' saying, "Love your enemies."
30. What effect would "loving our enemies" have upon us?
31. How did Buddha teach the same doctrine?
32. How did Paul describe Karma and Christ?
33. What great lessons does the law of action impress upon us?

CHAPTER VI.

REINCARNATION.

> "Our birth is but a sleep and a forgetting;
> The soul that rises with us, our life's star
> Hath had elsewhere its setting,
> And cometh from afar.
> Not in entire forgetfulness,
> And not in utter nakedness
> But trailing clouds of glory do we come
> From God who is our home."—*Wordsworth.*

> "The doctrine of metempsychosis may almost claim to be a natural or innate belief in the human mind, if we may judge from its wide diffusion among the nations of the earth and its prevalence throughout the historical ages"
> —*Prof. Francis Bowen.*

Closely connected with Karma, the law of action, is Reincarnation, or the rebirth of the same individual soul in a series of personalities. These latter are like the various costumes or characters played by the same actor on successive nights. One night he may impersonate Othello, another Romeo, and a third, Hamlet, but remains the same actor throughout. The permanent individuality, or soul, recollects the characters previously assumed, although the brain of this personality may be ignorant of their details.

Reincarnation provides the means for Karma to express itself; it is a universal law, as the "lives" are constantly passing from form to form, dying out of some to be reborn into others. All nature teaches this lesson of reëmbodiment, for continual change characterizes every visible object. Minerals break up through rust and corrosion, plants and animals are subject to growth and decay. As the matter of which these things are composed is indestructible, it must be reborn in new objects. Continual growth followed by decay is nature's method for providing progress for the "lives," which pass through alternating periods of activity and rest.

The Life sleeps in the seed, to wake in the plant, casting aside the old form of the seed to assume that of the plant. It sleeps in the tree during winter, to awake in the spring to build a new body in the fresh growth of foliage, bark and wood. In this new body it dwells during the summer, developing buds for future growth. The foliage helps the tree in growing, but when the autumn is over it drops off. In the same manner these bodies assist man's development, and when one period is ended they are cast off, which process is termed death; but it is no more death to us than the falling of leaves in autumn is death to the trees. Vegetation rests during the winter preparing for the succeeding summer's rebirth, and when our bodies are laid aside, we too rest before returning in new bodies for the growth of another earth life. Each season's growth is made from the buds formed during the previous summer; analogously we are dominated by the mental and physical tendencies of previous lives. If the buds are poor, the growth will be dwarfed, and if good it will result luxuriantly.

The life of the caterpillar illustrates reincarnation. Emerging from an egg, it grows rapidly and then weaves itself into a cocoon, assuming an entirely different shape ; from this it emerges a lovely butterfly. The same centre of life assumes four distinct changes within a short time, egg, caterpillar, chrysalis and butterfly. Man also passes through great vicissitudes during many lives, and even in the same life changes the body several times, as molecules continually leave it to be replaced by others.

Each year the tree trunk is encircled by another ring, and similarly each earth life adds a new experience to the human soul, where it is retained eternally.

There is no difficulty in tracing reëmbodiment as operating in the lower kingdoms, in which everything is continually decaying and being restored to the elements to serve as material for new forms; but there are some who question whether it rules among humanity. Does man live many times on earth? This raises the point as to what man is; whether he is the body or something within?

We have seen that the One Life is all-pervading and divided into many "lives" or souls, each of which is pursuing its evolution by assuming and then discarding material forms. The essence is identical in mineral, vegetable, animal and human beings, as these divisions designate the stages of development in physical evolution of the "lives" or souls within.

The "lives" are distinct from the forms which they inhabit, as the forces in minerals, plants and animals are distinct from their outer garments, which endure for a time and are then destroyed. In the same manner the soul in man is distinct from the body it uses for a time. The real man is not the body, but the soul, and it is this latter which is the permanent principle which reincarnates.

Minerals, plants, and animals, may have no recollection of prior conditions, but if evolution be true, their indestructible essence must have existed many times in various forms. Man may not remember his former bodies and their surroundings, but that is no disproof of previous lives. In the soul are stored past memories which may or may not be communicated to this brain. Many persons claim to possess recollections of the details of former lives, and as greater attention is being drawn to reincarnation in this Western world, evidence regarding it is accumulating.

Can Life die? Life is a force which may be transmuted but not extinguished, for such is a rule relating to forces. If the law of "conservation of energy" be applied to the soul or the "lives," those energies which cause manifestation, it is evident they cannot be extinguished, however many changes they may pass through.

The soul of man equally with the soul of all things in nature is immortal and indestructible, without a beginning and infinite as regards the future, but all alike take on many temporary and destructible bodies.

The theory that man has but one life on earth fails to give any explanation of the purpose of existence; its adherents admit this, for they suppose the soul to be created out of nothing at the birth of the body, and at death it proceeds either to a monotonous heaven, or a hell, the very existence of which finds few believers.

The purpose of life is clearly defined in the Bible as "Be ye perfect," and the same lesson is taught by the evolution of nature which exhibits everything progressing to a higher state by the coöperation of the "lives"; it is the lesson equally of our experience, for beginning with childhood we attend school and college, and later acquire knowledge and experience in our occupations, every one holding some ideal which he strives to attain.

The question arises, do we acquire perfection in one life? If not, reincarnation is a necessity. "To be perfect even as our Father in Heaven is perfect" requires that we possess all knowledge and all experience of every age, past and future, for nothing can be missing from perfection; also our characters must be purified of all sensuous and selfish impulses. Is it possible in one life to acquire this? All will admit that this is impossible, for the future is not yet within our reach. But some may suggest that this perfection is gained after death without return to this world. Unfortunately there is no proof of this, and the whole analogy of nature contradicts it. Such a suggestion deprives this life of any purpose—unless it be that man may sin and so give God an excuse for punishing him,—since the perfection is to be acquired after this life is over.

The question arises as to the locality of man's

previous and future lives; some may suggest a far-off planet as the bourne when the troubles of this life are over, and that there is no return to this world.

In studying the law regulating the lower kingdoms, we saw that past experience or Karma draws back the "lives" to embodiment according to the affinities in each one, working along the lines of the least resistance. Since man's actions are performed in company with others, and affect them to a greater or less degree, and as many of their effects are not exhausted in this present life, a return to meet former friends and enemies is necessary for purposes of adjustment.

If the law of Karma be true, there can be no chance or accident, or mere coincidence in daily happenings. Meetings with people for the first time in this life, in which we confer or receive benefits or harm, must result from meetings in former lives. Where more likely did we formerly meet, than in this world, the scene of our present evolution?

Every force re-acts upon the centre from which it originated, and as we are now under the influence of reactions in this world, probability points to this world as the place of their origin. Paul wrote "Whatsoever a man soweth, that shall he also reap." We cannot sow wheat in Venus and reap it in America; the present reaping is a crop springing from seeds sown in former lives. How else can we understand the different conditions of birth of each one? A child attends school for a few hours daily, returning to the same class day after day until ready for promotion to a more advanced one. Man must continue to reincarnate upon this earth until all experience has been acquired which this world can afford. As Karma is the schoolmaster, this world is the schoolhouse.

The law of reincarnation coupled with Karma, the doctrine of justice, is the only explanation of the enigmas of life. The same souls now incarnated in bodies—perhaps ourselves—have for interminable ages been helping to mould the conditions of the world and make history, and are now enjoying or suffering for such past deeds. Nothing else can explain the great problem of Good and Evil, and reconcile man to the seeming injustice of life. When one observes inequalities of birth, station, intellect and health, the deserving loaded down with hardships, and the idle and profligate in the enjoyment of bounties, nothing but reliance upon these fixed laws can give confidence in the existence of justice as ruling in the universe.

Reincarnation is the only explanation of the attributes of immortality and divinity in man, and is an inestimable comfort in providing a means for becoming perfect, even as our Father in Heaven (the One Life) is perfect.

QUESTIONS ON CHAPTER VI.

1. What is the meaning of reincarnation?
2. How does an actor illustrate reincarnation?
3. What relation does reincarnation bear to karma?
4. Is the principle of reëmbodiment universal in Nature? Give reasons.

5. Describe the process of reincarnation as applied to the "lives"; also to trees.

6. How does a caterpillar illustrate reincarnation?

7. Explain how the analogy of Nature points to reincarnation in man.

8. What reincarnates in the lower kingdoms?

9. What reincarnates in man?

10. Do minerals, plants, and animals, recollect former lives?

11. How do we know they have existed before?

12. If man has no recollection, why is that no disproof of reincarnation?

13. Why do we not recollect details of former lives?

14. What is Life? Can it die? Why not?

15. What does "conservation of energy" mean?

16. How does the soul in man resemble and differ from the souls in the lower kingdoms?

17. What is the popular idea of the past and future of the soul?

18. How does the Bible define the purpose of life?

19. Can this be reached in one life on earth? Give reasons.

20. Why must we reincarnate on this world, and not on some other planet?

21. What governs daily happenings, and the benefits or harm we confer or receive?

22. How does reincarnation explain different conditions?

23. What purpose does the world fulfil as regards mankind?

24. Is there any other explanation of the enigmas of life?

25. What have our souls been doing in the past?

26. What effect do karma and reincarnation have upon our minds?

27. How does man become perfect?

28. What is perfection?

We are our own children.—*Pythagoras.*

He needed not the spectacles of books to read nature; he looked inwards and found her there.—*Dryden.*

Think not that I am come to destroy the law, or the prophets. I am not come to destroy, but to fulfil.—*Matth. V.*

Our human laws are but the copies, more or less imperfect, of the eternal laws so far as we can read them, and either succeed and promote our welfare, or fail and bring confusion and disaster, according as the legislators' insight has detected the true principle, or has been distorted by ignorance or selfishness.—*Froude.*

We can drive a stone upward for a moment into the air, but it is yet true that all stones will forever fall; and whatever instances can be quoted of unpunished theft, or of a lie which somebody credited, justice must prevail, and it is the privilege of truth to make itself believed. Character is this moral order seen through the medium of an individual nature.—*Emerson.*

CHAPTER VII.

PROGRESS.

> "Heaven is not reached at a single bound;
> But we build the ladder by which we rise
> From the lowly earth to the vaulted skies,
> And we mount to its summit, round by round."
> —*J. G. Holland.*

> "Older than all preached gospels was this unpreached, inarticulate, but ineradicable, forever-enduring gospel: work, and therein have well-being. Man, son of earth and of heaven, lies there not, in the innermost heart of thee, a spirit of active method, a force for work, that burns like a painfully mouldering fire, giving thee no rest till thou unfold it, till thou write it down in beneficent facts around thee?"—*T. Carlyle.*

Since all "lives" are sparks of the One Life, however small and dim, they possess the characteristics of that Life with its possibilities of unfoldment and progress in evolution. "Everything evinces a progressive march towards a higher life. There is design in the action of seemingly blindest forces." The laws of "natural selection" and "survival of the fittest" which seem so cruel are working towards the grand end of progress.

The object of existence is for progressive development, which flows as a necessary result from the presence and activity of the One Life, for it is coöperative in its methods. Every race of mankind has had a dim recognition of this coöperation or spirit of helpfulness in nature, the loftiest attribute of divinity; and it has led many to offer prayers and entreaties for help to higher powers under various symbols and names.

Former lessons have dealt with the relation that all outer things bear to the divine in nature, to God, to the One Life,—that in the soul all are inseparably connected as parts of it. Terrestrial existence is for the soul's experience and not as many think, to pamper the body by gratification of its selfish impulses.

The soul assumes a body at birth in exact accord with its own past, and after accomplishing its life's work, withdraws from that instrument which returns to the elements; but the soul lives on. Prayers and entreaties to God to infringe His own laws in favor of individual suppliants are manifestly useless.

We should not despise any life because it seems small, for all is divine and there is no limit to what it may become. Minerals are transformed into beautiful flowers. From a tiny egg emerges a caterpillar that occupies its life in eating, then wrapping itself in a protecting coat for a sleep, awakens a lovely butterfly. A thing of earth becomes a denizen of the air.

Progress is continual. The end of one cycle marks the beginning for another. During the existence of worlds, the great *heart* of nature, the One Life, is ever pulsing out its helpful force under the immutable law which is Eternal Motion, cyclic and spiral, and therefore progressive. The bud proceeds from the seed, and the flower from the bud, developing form, color and odor, and then these die down and disappear, leaving but another seed for the coming season.

The chambered nautilus is a beautiful illustration of the same truth. The spiral shell shows how year by year it built upon itself newer and larger mansions as the old were outgrown. The door of the old growth was closed behind, but the shell was carried with it as the embodiment of its past history, a type of all growth.

Souls or "lives" accumulate past experiences, but are ever constructing new coverings to suit growing needs. When they reached the human stage, the bodies of the animal kingdom no longer served for their progress. The old animal house was outgrown, its experience had been already gained, and therefore the door of the animal kingdom was closed for reincarnation of human souls. For all the great march is onward, for the One Life is ever actively forcing forward everything by the help that each life is obliged to render its brother life. For this vital force directs growth, makes the seed germinate and forms trunk and branches, which in their turn produce other trees. This is the never-dying breath of life.

Progress is everywhere, ruling in worlds and universes as well as in all the beings they contain, down to the smallest atoms.

This lesson of progress is quite in accord with every-day experience. The child attends school to acquire education, and spends the greater part of his after life in gaining dexterity and additional experience in some chosen vocation, by consciously striving toward some ideal. Nature has set out her landmarks very clearly, the mineral, vegetable, animal and human kingdoms representing progressive stages in development. There are a definite number of "lives" or souls in each kingdom, and although they may temporarily ascend to a higher one, they return home upon the disintegration of the form in which they were embodied.

Each department of nature is an initiation over the one below, advance from one to another occupying many millions of years. After a long period of activity, the world passes through an equal period of rest, as sleeping follows the waking state. When the world awakens from one of these states of rest, the aspiring "lives" of each kingdom have advanced a step in evolution. Those which in the previous cycle occupied mineral forms are now advanced to the vegetable, and the former vegetable "lives" are now animating animals, and the animal become vehicles for use by human souls. As the Kabala expresses this orderly progression, "The stone becomes a plant, the plant an animal, the animal a man and the man a God;"—or, as the Hindus say, "God sleeps in the stone, breathes in the plant, moves in the animal and wakes to consciousness in the man."

Progress in nature follows a fixed law, the law of the One Life. We get help by giving help. This rule applies to all stages of evolution in each kingdom of nature. In a former lesson it was shown how plants grow and fashion themselves by raising the minerals to the vegetable kingdom, and everywhere the higher "lives" build new tenements by using those in a less progressed state and thus raise them. The bee aids the plant by distributing pollen, and receives aid in return. Information imparted to another sinks more deeply into our own mind;—in the act of giving we arrive at a fuller knowledge. Advance in evolution is made by the higher "lives" descending into lower kingdoms, by embodying themselves in, or taking on coverings of the lower, and thus infusing them with their own more advanced development. Advance takes place by the higher lifting up the lower, for the latter cannot raise themselves; this is illustrated by the seed breaking up minerals and incorporating them in the plant. Without this help the minerals would not be able to fashion the plant. This great law of nature is the basis of the dogmas of the vicarious atonement and the crucifixion. The immortal soul (the Christ) enters human bodies to save them, that is to raise them to a divine state. This operation goes on eternally, as higher entities, out of their compassion, embody themselves among the lower, crucifying themselves in the act, to assist the less progressed and become the vicarious sacrifice for the sins of the lower. The souls thus voluntarily crucified by the trials of daily life are rewarded by the wisdom gained in the experiences of this life. It is a universal law that help is gained in proportion as it is given.

The human soul acquired its individuality prior to becoming the present humanity. It has the task of conquering the instincts and desires of the animal body in which it dwells, by the use of the thinking and reasoning faculties of the mind. This conquest must be achieved by each one through the conscious use of will power.

Man has the endowment of free will, able to follow selfish impulses of the animal body, or to listen to the guidance of the soul. The former are selfish, bringing suffering in their train, for injury to others carries exact retribution ; we reap as we sow.

Life by life the experience gained through suffering brings self-control, enabling us to refrain when tempted. Through suffering the will grows stronger, character is gained and there is a gradual extinction of selfish desire and loosening of its hold over the mind.

Repentance and forgiveness are explained by the law of Karma and form an important step in progress. The commission of sins is followed by suffering as the penalty ; but suffering gradually leads to repentance, a " turning away from " the repetition of the offence, as the desire to sin loosens its hold upon the mind. When thorough repentance is reached, that we sin no more, restitution for past offences can be made, and forgiveness is obtained. " With whatsoever measure ye mete, it shall be measured to you again." Wh ɩ· we sin, suffering will be ours. Only by rep ɩ. tance or turning away from our faults can finɑ. forgiveness be reached. For instance, a person may be rich, but use his wealth selfishly to gratify bodily lusts or personal ambition, and thus form in his mind a strong attachment to riches for the means of selfish gratification they offer. This wrongful use may cause such a person to be reborn many times into a state of poverty wherein the mind, by the sufferings endured, may gradually be purged of the selfish attachment to wealth. When the mind is purified of these selfish tendencies, a state of repentance is reached, and riches, with the power of helping others which accompanies them, may be restored to the repentant sinner. We must cease committing injuries and hating others, and by helping them set right old scores and thus gain forgiveness, recollecting that the lesson of the One Life is that all must render help, whereas injury and hatred are impediments to man's progression. We advance by helping other and less advanced entities, for the law of Brotherhood holds good wherever the One Life is in operation. The more progressed the state of evolution, the greater the power possessed by the entity to render help to others. Man in his highest development thus becomes Godlike, a powerful agent for the dissemination of the beneficent forces of the One Life. He carries help to all forms in the lower kingdoms, raising and advancing them, and in greater measure is able to assist his fellow man by evoking the soul within him. Thus is salvation obtained from the almost irresistible dictates of animal propensities and from the woe and misery they entail.

Progress in its highest attainment is reached by perfect purity of thought, word and deed, represented by entire unselfishness; for thus we learn to live in harmony with the Absolute Unity, that ever pulsating heart that beats throughout every form of the One Life.

QUESTIONS ON CHAPTER VII.

1. How do the One Life and the "lives" exhibit progress?
2. How do "natural selection" and the "survival of the fittest" operate toward progress?
3. What proof is there that all races have recognized Nature's coöperative action?
4. Is the popular conception of God derived from the One Life? Give reasons.
5. Trace the history of a soul during one incarnation.
6. Why are selfish prayers useless?
7. Why should we refrain from despising life in minor objects?
8. Has progress any limit? Give reasons.
9. What part in progress have destruction and decay?
10. How does the nautilus illustrate progress?
11. What part has the soul in progress?
12. Why cannot human souls reincarnate in animals?
13. What is the ultimate cause of progress? Explain how this operates.
14. How do our daily lives teach progress?
15. How is progress depicted in the kingdoms of nature?
16. Are the "lives" attached to the separate kingdoms?
17. When do "lives" progress to a higher kingdom?

18. Can the "lives" ascend to a higher kingdom in the present cycle?

19. Describe the progression of the "lives" to a higher kingdom.

20. Define the law underlying progress.

21. Is this law universally applicable?

22. How do plants illustrate the law of helpfulness?

23. In what manner does teaching another help the teacher?

24. What is necessary for "lives" to advance to a higher kingdom?

25. Can "lives" raise themselves to higher kingdoms?

26. How does this law explain the dogmas of vicarious atonement and the crucifixion?

27. How are "lives" compensated for raising lower ones?

28. When did the human soul become individualized?

29. What is the task of the soul in human bodies?

30. Upon what does the soul act to accomplish this task?

31. What does free will enable man to do?

32. What is the purpose of suffering?

33. Explain repentance and forgiveness.

34. Describe the effect of selfishness upon us and how repentance is reached.

35. How can man become an active part of the One Life?

36. What is man's highest goal?

37. What are essential to progress?

CHAPTER VIII.

DUALITY.

> "Polarity, or action and reaction, we meet in every part of nature. . . . . An inevitable dualism bisects nature. . . . . Whilst the world is dual, so is every one of its parts."—*Emerson.*

> "All actions performed other than as sacrifice unto God make the actor bound by action. . . . . He who seeks nothing and nothing rejects, being free from the influence of the 'pairs of opposites,' without trouble he is released from the bonds forged by action."—*Bhagavac-Gita.*

The whole of nature is pervaded by duality. The One Life has visible and invisible aspects; its transitory forms and their permanent foundations. Every cycle is made up of two opposites, as activity and rest, cause and effect, sleeping and waking, life and death, ebb and flow, pleasure and pain, loving and hating. A "pair of opposites" consists of two aspects of one thing, which arise in our consciousness as the result of the operations of mind.

In the present stage of evolution, man is perfecting the mental faculties. Through perception he is enabled to compare and contrast things with their opposites, eliminate errors and correct his judgments, until ultimately he reaches knowledge. The dual aspect of all things is a stage of mental growth through which all pass, for it affords experience of both sides. Without perception of pain, we cannot value pleasure; experience of cold is necessary to appreciate what heat is; a person born blind cannot judge between light and darkness, having no basis for comparison.

As attachment of the mind to, or desire for either opposite is lost, we become equal minded in pleasure and pain, and true knowledge is acquired of the Unity underlying seeming duality.

In nature's workshop, duality rules. Take plant life ; there the single cell divides, building another on itself, growth being the continued repetition of this dual activity. When the expanding bud within the seed bursts the outer coat, it sends a root downward into the earth, and a stalk upward into the air and sunlight. Each of these opposites is necessary for the plant to perfect itself. The purpose of the dual expression is experience and growth for each manifestation of life. The plant needs roots for the help they render in the darkness of the earth, and also leaves and branches for gaining assistance from air and sunshine. While stillness and warmth help the oak tree in growing, tempest and cold make its fibre strong.

Throughout manifested nature can be traced the positive and negative principles, each necessary and complementary to the other. There is the thought and its embodiment, the ideal in the sculptor's brain and its materialization in marble. Wherever objective forms are found, there is duality ; for instance, the tree and the life within ; the animal and its vital principle ; the human body and its soul. Everything which has an outer shape in this world, has its unseen basis in the One Life.

Man possesses two natures, which we may name higher and lower, and which give rise to a dual set of motives. The lower, including the body and its instincts, furnishes the vehicle for operations in this world and for gathering experience; but the helpful influence of the higher nature is necessary for this experience to become real progress.

Animal instincts must be controlled, and trained to conform to the higher will, enabling the body to serve as a useful instrument for conveying to others the beneficent help of the One Life. In such case all the "lives" of which the lower nature is composed will be purified and elevated.

To comprehend good and evil has been a long-standing problem. They are a "pair of opposites" explained by the duality of nature. Neither of them has a permanent existence, but each represents the impression made upon us by our surroundings. These impressions may seem good or evil, pleasant or unpleasant for the moment, but their effect constantly varies as our mental attitude changes. When Karma is realized as a fact—that everything happens as the result of our own former deeds—we no longer try to evade the inevitable, but face the lessons of life and learn contentment therein. Former evils will then cease impressing us as such, unpleasant events may occur, but we may acquire the power of being unmoved by them, and they will not affect us prejudicially. In past incarnations good and evil actions have attached us to others, for hatred as well as love is a cause of attachment;

now we meet with the results in the mixed good and evil of life. We may stop the recurrence of the evil in the future, by refraining now from returning evil with evil, or hatred with hatred, and learning to practise the difficult injunction given by Jesus of "loving our enemies" and helping those who persecute and injure us. The power to succeed in this, requires us to be "equal minded toward friend and foe," and in such case evil ceases to be unpleasant, for we have risen to a mental state where good and evil are treated philosophically. It is sometimes necessary to appear harsh, and exercise restraint over the actions of others for their own good, as a mother must restrain a child. This restraint seems at the time to be evil, but it is prompted by love. Good and evil are but changing incidents in a life of change.

Taking the One Life as our ideal and striving to become a co-worker with it, we see that it is the great beneficent providence, every part rendering help to other parts. By assisting those around us, exercising true charity without any desire for personal reward, the motive becomes purified, the heart bursts the bonds of the selfish mind, and we rise above the effects of good and evil events. Every such effort causes veils to fall away from the mind, and the soul gains power to guide us, and we become more powerful agents for the One Life to carry out its purpose of helping everything. Then the great heart of nature vibrates in us, having awakened a sympathetic chord which unites us to the whole.

The dual set of motives in us arises from the impulses of the body and soul affecting the mind. The body with its senses, vitality and instincts impels to selfishness, for its existence as a body is limited to the present life, without past or future; its tendencies are to gain satisfaction of its desires, lusts and cravings. The body would be deprived of some indulgence were we to practise charity, or give something to another. The soul or spiritual nature instigates to unselfish living; it is part of the One Life, eternal and infinite, conscious that the same life pervades everything, and it perceives no separateness or distinction between itself and others. The impulse of the soul is to be charitable and helpful, brotherly, loving and compassionate toward all beings. Its view is not narrowed by the horizon of this present life, but widened to include the ties of all past lives.

A person may be termed atheist, agnostic or pagan, and may deny the existence of any God or spiritual realm, yet his thoughts and actions as far as they are compassionate and brotherly are prompted by the soul, even if he profess to be unconscious of its existence.

Compassion and kindness are innate in the vast majority. In the face of some great calamity or danger, this innate kindness springs to the surface and asserts itself spontaneously, forming the closest of bonds and causing frantic efforts to be made to render assistance. At times we permit selfish instincts to cloud the nobler ones of the soul, and fear creeps in to paralyze us. Fear is the result of ignorance, the effect of the animal consciousness upon the brain mind, which compares and contrasts perceptions, but lacks confidence in its conclusions. The result of fear is seen in the case of a man falling into deep water. If not practised in swimming, the mind paralyzes his efforts with fear, and he sinks. The practised swimmer has confidence, dominates the lower mind and swims ashore. Likewise an animal, following its instincts, swims naturally the first time it enters the water.

The uncontrolled mind, dominated by selfish motives, suggests doubts, worries and anxieties and other forms of fear, which cause us to suffer in anticipation of events which may never occur. Fear does not exist in the soul, for the latter knows without reasoning and possesses the courage of its convictions. The soul knows itself to be part of the One Life, is invulnerable and indestructible. In the words of the Bhagavad Gita, Chapter II., "I myself never was not, nor thou, nor all the princes of the earth ; nor shall we ever hereafter cease to be."

While the soul inhabits a body, evil cannot be avoided, for the limitations of material surroundings are the causes of that which seems evil. The only good is in Unity, but the mind influenced by the pairs of opposites becomes attached to the dual results of actions, favorable or unfavorable, and is enslaved. The soul must burst these bonds and be free, in order to reach true happiness. The mind subject to bodily senses is unable to discriminate clearly ; hence the lack of reliability of human judgments. Not being free ourselves from the liability to err, how can we legitimately condemn others? In all human relations this thought should lead to the greatest toleration towards others' faults. We are not acquainted with the causes which led to the commission of that which we condemn; hence, however strongly we may disapprove of the offense, the offender should be free from condemnation by us. The law of the One Life is just, and will see that justice is meted out. Judgments and condemnations of others are beyond our rightful jurisdiction; hence we have no right to take life for life. "Vengeance is mine, I will repay," saith the Lord.

Present materialistic civilization appeals mainly to the senses, holding in highest esteem ostentatious living and lavish expenditure. Through the senses our minds become slaves to the pairs of opposites—pleasure and pain, good and evil, "which come and go and are brief and changeable." Present conditions directly conduce to suffering, unrest and disturbance, but are teaching the lesson of control in the mind over these selfish impulses. When the emptiness of personal ambition, vanity, place and power is acknowledged, they will be replaced by less selfish motives, for the results of the former will be lost when the body dies, leaving naught but a legacy of future suffering.

The wise man endeavors to reach the spot in his own heart where he ceases to be subject to the disturbing influence of this duality. It is in us all. This is the meaning of the terms "finding the Christ," and "the kingdom of Heaven is within," and is treated at length in "The Voice of the Silence."

These temporary bodies are but envelopes for the soul; bodily impulses must be restrained by understanding the nature and laws of the soul. The Bhagavad Gita, the Bible of the Hindus, says of the soul, Chap. II.: "It is eternal, universal, permanent, immovable; it is invisible, inconceivable, and unalterable."

Dwelling in thought upon the soul's attributes, and studying the teachings of Jesus in their inner meaning, or the "Bhagavad Gita," or other sacred books, brings a realization of the divine part of ourselves. This knowledge strengthens in the hour of temptation, and gives us power to control the passions; for the soul is part of the One Life, receiving help from other souls, unless we choose to close the doors. The most effective manner of gaining help in our struggles is to give help, for thus are the doors of help opened and we become co-workers with the One Life.

QUESTIONS ON CHAPTER VIII.

1. How is duality in nature perceived?
2. Give illustrations of duality.
3. What causes "pairs of opposites"?
4. What is man now perfecting?
5. Explain how the mind operates.
6. How is true knowledge acquired?
7. Illustrate duality in nature.
8. Illustrate duality in mental spheres.

9. Illustrate duality in man.
10. Describe the lower and higher natures in man.
11. What is the rightful relation between the personality and the soul?
12. What are good and evil?
13. From what do they arise?
14. Why do good and evil interchange?
15. What effect has the knowledge of the law of Karma upon us?
16. Can we change evil into good? Describe.
17. Can we evade good and evil happenings?
18. Can we avoid the recurrence of evil in the future? Describe.
19. How do we form future attachments to others by hatred?
20. How can these attachments be overcome?
21. What is the lesson of the One Life?
22. How can motives be purified?
23. How do the two sets of motives arise in us?
24. Why are the motives of the body selfish?
25. Why are the motives of the soul unselfish?
26. Whence spring compassion and love in an agnostic or atheist?
27. Are compassion and kindness innate in humanity? Illustrate.
28. What is the effect of fear upon the mind?
29. Of what is it the result?
30. Illustrate the result of fear upon man and animals.
31. What suggests doubts, worries and anxieties respecting events which never happen?

DUALITY.

32. How can anxiety be avoided?
33. What is the cause of evil?
34. How can happiness be reached?
35. Why should we not condemn others?
36. Why should we be tolerant of others' faults?
37. Explain why criminals cannot escape their just deserts.
38. What is the effect of our present conditions?
39. What does "finding the Christ" mean?
40. How can we gain faith in the existence of the soul?

> " Nature never did betray
> The heart that loved her; 't is her privilege,
> Through all the years of this our life, to lead
> From joy to joy: for she can so inform
> The mind that is within us, so impress
> With quietness and beauty, and so feed
> With lofty thoughts, that neither evil tongues,
> Rash judgments, nor the sneers of selfish men,
> Nor greetings where no kindness is, nor all
> The dreary intercourse of daily life
> Shall e'er prevail against us."—*Wordsworth.*

> "—— Still somehow the round
> Is spiral, and the races' feet have found
> The path rise under them which they have trod"
> —*Wm. Dean Howells.*

"Thou shalt not let thy senses make a playground of thy mind."

"Thou shalt not separate thy being from BEING, and the rest, but merge the Ocean in the drop, the drop within the Ocean."

"So shalt thou be in full accord with all that lives; bear love to men as though they were thy brother pupils, disciples of one Teacher, the sons of one sweet Mother."

"Compassion speaks and saith; Can there be bliss when all that lives must suffer? Shalt thou be saved and hear the whole world cry?"—*Voice of the Silence.*

CHAPTER IX.

SEVENFOLD MANIFESTATION.

> "These appearances indicate the fact that the universe is represented in every one of its particles. Everything in nature contains all the powers of nature."—*Emerson.*
>
> "A careful analysis, however, reduces these infinite potencies and potentialities to seven great divisions, which in man are classed as Principles, and in the cosmos as Hierarchies."
> —*J. A. Anderson, M.D.*

The One Life pulses through infinite space, manifesting itself on seven planes of being. These planes are not separated from each other in space, but each of them is everywhere; they interpenetrate and interblend. This interblending may be illustrated by a bowl of water in which are placed coloring matter, salt and other ingredients, and heat applied to it. The water, color, salt and heat are separate in themselves, but interblend with each other, and each is found permeating the others.

The seven different planes or conditions in which the One Life manifests itself are called the sevenfold manifestation. They have a regular order and sequence, although interblended.

Considered as rates of vibration, these planes begin with the most rapid and descend step by step through seven gradations to the slowest. If applied to matter, the planes commence with the most ethereal substance, passing through seven stages, each more material than the preceding, to the most dense—that of this earth.

That matter of different densities will interpenetrate is illustrated by the every-day experience of electricians. The same cable will convey several messages simultaneously from New York to Europe and *vice versa*, provided currents of electricity of varying strengths be employed. The different currents pass and repass through each other without interference.

The recent revelations with the X-rays show that matter can pass through other matter. Photographs of a human body have been taken through clothing, a plate of glass, and a piece of wood several inches in thickness. Respecting this, Nikola Tesla, the great electrician, writes: "I am getting more and more convinced that we have to deal with a stream of particles which strike the sensitive plate with great velocities." In this case, particles of the human frame must have penetrated the various intervening obstacles.

There are around us seven globes of matter of different densities, and man possesses seven natures or principles corresponding with these globes, enabling him to act upon them all. As the seed contains the whole plant from the roots to the blossom in a latent state, so does the One Life contain its sevenfold manifestation, itself being upon the highest plane. Upon proceeding to pass from the invisible state to assume a form, the lives pass downward through the seven planes until the lowest, that of physical manifestation, is reached.

The sevenfold manifestation characterizes everything around us. A ray of light divides into the seven colors of the prismatic scale, the same order being invariable, from the violet, the most rapid vibration, by a gradually descending scale to the red. What better illustration of this can there be than the rainbow? Sound divides into seven tones, and the piano into a series of octaves, the difference between treble and bass being a lessening of the rates of vibration. Chemical elements form into groups of seven according to their atomic weights. Man has seven senses, two not yet fully developed. Seven is the dominating number, as witnessed in the phases of the moon, and periods of seven in diseases and gestation. Seven rules in the formation of the body, which has seven skins, etc. The seven days of the week and the seven sacred planets are connected with this fact.

The One Life is always the same in essence, its seven diverse appearances depending upon the vehicle it uses. If a lamp be covered with seven globes, varying in density, the radiation of light will vary with the opaqueness of the globes.

The One Life acting in man assumes seven different expressions. Four of these are temporary, and three are permanent. The four lower may be written around a square as follows:

Desire.

Physical life.   Astral mould or form body.

Body.

The lowest and most dense is the physical body, the outer garment. The body in itself is senseless, for when sleeping it can neither see nor hear. It has sense organs, but these cannot act unless there is something within to use them.

This inner body acting directly upon the physical organs, is called the astral body, being of the same size and shape as the physical, but of finer matter, and visible only to the astral eyes. The astral body precedes the physical, the latter being built into it cell for cell. It varies very little during life, but acts as a pattern and model to preserve the shape of the physical body during the constant change of its particles. The senses of sight, hearing, smelling, etc., do not pertain to the physical body, but to the astral, which uses the outer organs as mechanical instruments to establish a means of communication between external nature and itself. Both physical and astral bodies are built of little "lives."

The next principle is physical life or vitality, pervading every part of the body and energizing the organs, using the astral body as its vehicle or channel.

The last principle of this quaternary is "desire," the force which makes us want things for ourselves, the basis of selfishness. Desire permeates the entire lower man, "and like the astral body may be added to or diminished, made weak or increased in strength, debased or purified."

"These four lower principles are common to man and animals, as well as to the vegetable kingdom, though in the last but faintly developed. At one period in evolution no further than the material principles had been developed; the three higher of mind, soul and spirit were but latent. Up to this point man and animal were equal, for the brute in us is made of the passions and the astral body."

The three higher principles, or triad, may be represented by a triangle:

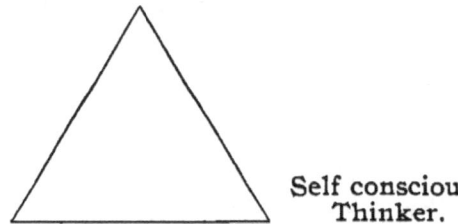

The Knower or perceiver conveys intelligence to us without thinking or reasoning. It is that feeling of conviction which assures us with certainty. It is the faculty of spiritual discernment.

The next principle is the Self-conscious Thinker, wherein the One Life perceives itself as Thinker. The Ray of the One Life acts through both these principles, through the one as Knower and the other as Thinker, and in the latter recognizes itself as such and is therefore called self-conscious.

The connecting ray between triangle and square is the thinking brain-mind, the subject of our next lesson.

This is the sevenfold manifestation of man's

nature, wherein all the principles interblend with each other, and permeate the whole body and beyond it for a space. The astral or nerve body is in every part of the physical form; the vitality, desire, mind, soul and spirit also interpenetrate each other.

The chain of seven globes of matter correspond with man's principles, and equally interblend, enabling the Ego or Thinker within us to act at different times on these several planes, by changing its consciousness from one to another. While the Ego acts through the physical body, it is conscious in this world, and recognizes its surroundings here; but when the body sleeps, it functions on the astral or other globe and recognizes its surroundings there, losing consciousness of this world for the time. Upon awakening, a return of consciousness is made to this world. Dreams are recollections brought from other planes and impressed upon the physical brain with sufficient force to be remembered after awakening. Even in waking hours the Ego passes to other planes, as when deeply absorbed in thought or work, or very strongly carried away by some desire, we forget present surroundings for the time. Death is very similar to sleep, for the Ego passes in consciousness from the physical body and loses touch with its surroundings in this world; but in the one case it returns upon awakening, and in the other it does not return to that body, but will come back in another upon reincarnation.

The sevenfold manifestation of man gives a

clear analysis of his nature. The One Life is universal in its character, the Infinite Deity. The next principle is the universal soul endowed with spiritual discernment; and the third, the individual soul in each human being. This individual soul, derived directly from the One Life, is in everyone, persisting from life to life and storing the experience gained. It is the reincarnating Ego, which has been compared to a silken thread upon which are strung the pearls of experience of each life. This is the real man who inhabits the body.

The four lower principles are but instruments used by the real man to enable him to come into contact with nature and his surroundings in this world, in order to know himself. Whenever an act is performed, the four lower principles transmute the thought of the Ego into the action. The thought becomes a desire, and is transmitted through the nerves or astral body, vitalized by the life principle, to the muscles, and the act is performed. If any one of these principles were deficient, the connection between the mental and physical planes would be severed, and an idiot would result. The square represents the mortal and impermanent part of man, which he uses for the one earth life and then discards. To live for the body and its desires alone is a waste of time, for at death the result of our efforts is lost. The body is the lowest, least important and most transitory of these principles. Deprived of the man within, the organs of the body are senseless and useless.

The sevenfold manifestation of the One Life shows how everything in nature is intimately associated, and each part is necessary to bind together and assist the whole. The great heart of the universe is one, but manifests in different manners.

QUESTIONS ON CHAPTER IX.

1. Describe how the One Life manifests on seven different planes.

2. How do you picture these planes?

3. Are the planes separate in space?

4. Can seven things fill the same space at the same time? Explain by bowl of water.

5. What is the basis of the order of the seven planes?

6. Explain these planes as related to (1) vibration; (2) matter.

7. Which plane is the most dense?

8. How does electricity demonstrate that matter can interpenetrate matter? Does the X-ray show this?

9. How does man correspond with the seven planes of the globe?

10. How does a seed illustrate the seven planes?

11. Name other examples of sevenfold manifestation.

12. Upon what do the seven different manifestations depend?

13. How many principles in man are temporary? Name them. What is a principle?

14. How do we perceive that the physical body in itself is senseless?

15. Describe the astral body.
16. Of what is the astral body composed?
17. What purposes does the astral body serve?
18. How can you show that the senses are in the astral body?
19. What is the nature of the next principle?
20. What is the fourth principle? Describe it.
21. What principles has the animal in common with man?
22. Name the three higher principles, the triad.
23. How do these differ from the four lower principles?
24. Describe the "Knower."
25. Name the next principle. Describe.
26. What is the connection between triangle and square?
27. Describe how the seven principles are interblended.
28. What enables man to change his state of consciousness? Illustrate.
29. What are dreams?
30. Analyze the triangle, showing relation of the reincarnating Ego to the One Life.
31. What purpose do the four lower principles (the square) serve? Analyze them.
32. What causes idiocy?
33. Why is it a mistake to live for bodily desires?
34. What moral lesson does the sevenfold manifestation afford?

CHAPTER X.

THE CONNECTING RAY.

"Life is but a means unto an end—that end,
Beginning, mean, and end of all things—God.
We live in deeds, not years; in thoughts, not breaths;
In feelings, not in figures on a dial.
We should count time by heart throbs. He most lives
Who thinks most, feels the noblest, acts the best."
—*Bailey.*

"For mind is like a mirror: it gathers dust while it reflects. It needs the gentle breezes of Soul-Wisdom to brush away the dust of our illusions. Seek, O Beginner, to blend thy Mind and Soul."
—*Voice of the Silence.*

At each incarnation of a human being, the self-conscious Thinker emanates a ray from itself which joins the real, immortal man to the personality of that incarnation, the soul to its body; this connecting ray is our thinking mind. The ray is an emanation from, or a reflection of, the higher mind into the lower vehicle, forming a bridge by which the human, thinking personality can mount upward and join the higher. The path is found by our aspiring to follow the law of the divine man.

The four lower principles of man's constitution were developed by evolution, forming the body of man with its desires and passions, with a brain more highly developed than that of any other animal. The personality, composed of the four lower principles, breaks up at death, and is reconstructed at rebirth, this being repeated from life to life until the personality is raised to the plane of the self-conscious Thinker through the illumination of the ray, and a permanent, immortal entity is formed.

The connecting ray between Spirit and personality was supplied by individual Souls who incarnated a ray from themselves into the mindless men. These Souls had gained self-consciousness ages ago in other worlds and systems of worlds, in previous evolutionary periods, which were completed before the solar system existed.

The manner in which this light of mind was given to the mindless men can be illustrated by one candle lighting many. The expanded brain of the mindless beings was like a candle fully formed and with wick prepared, but not yet lighted. As from one lighted candle numerous unlighted ones can be set aflame, so the illuminating Souls, called the "Sons of Wisdom," lit up the animal man by enlightening his mind, which he was unable to do without this assistance. The "Sons of Wisdom" are the Elder Brothers of every family of men on any globe, and have derived the light from others who reach back and back in endless procession without beginning or end. It is thus by receiving Their light that each race is prepared for final initiation.

The reincarnating Ego, or individual Soul, is immortal, accumulating and carrying the results of experience from life to life. This Ego assumes two aspects upon entering a body; there is the intuitional faculty which knows, and the reasoning, which works through the brain-mind. This reasoning faculty is a superior organism which the Thinker uses to reach its conclusions, and creates man's superiority to animals, for the latter act from automatic or instinctual impulses.

Desire, the predominant characteristic of animals, is nearest to the reasoning aspect of the Ego, and usually brings a strong influence to bear upon it; whereas the intuitional has affinity for spiritual things. If the tendencies are wholly intellectual, the individual tends downward; for intellect is cold, heartless and selfish unless lit up by the spiritual flame. With every effort of will toward purification and unity with this inner Self-God, one of the ties binding it to the lower breaks, and the spiritual entity of man is drawn higher until eventually he is absorbed into the highest beam of the Parent Sun.

In the brain-mind is the battle-field of the contending forces, for man must by his own self-conscious effort lift himself mentally out of the controlling influence of worldly temptations. In the mind alone can St. George slay the Dragon, for it is here that the fight must take place. This connecting ray is our self, which exercises the power of choice to follow either the selfish animal passions, or the guidance of the divine by slaying the Dragon. When we follow the higher intuition, we may be said to have reached the end of the rainbow, and to have found that spiritual wisdom which is symbolized by the pot of gold.

The "War in Heaven" allegorizes the contest between the two opposing forces in man. This war will last till the inner and divine adjusts his outer terrestrial self to his own spiritual nature. Till then the fierce and dark passions will be at continual feud with their master, the Divine Man. But the animal will be tamed one day, because its nature will be changed, and harmony will reign once more.

The connecting ray is our thinking mind, wherein we are usually centred. It is the tie between the square and the triangle, subject to the impulses of both. Everyone is conscious of being tempted by the one, yet feels the higher trying to induce him not to yield. It is not always easy to obey the higher, on account of mental habits; but the hard struggle must be persisted in, for man must save himself from falling. He is a complex creature in whom reside these two forces, so difficult to be harmonized. The history of a life is the story of the swaying influences of the animal and the God. The evidence of the animal nature is written at times on the features. On some is the cunning of the fox, never directly approaching its ends, but adopting indirect, underhand methods; in others, cruelty, disregard of the rights of their fellows, obstinacy, treachery or greed. On the other hand, there are the noble and self-sacrificing natures which make their owners but a little lower than the angels, before whom one instinctively bows. Even the humblest and dullest has in some dark corner of himself all these godlike possibilities.

Between these two natures, man himself, the connecting ray, stands. He is the monarch for the present life, with absolute power of choice. Like the man at the wheel, he can steer whatever course he may choose, being guided by the God within, or allowing the animal to hold the rudder; but if the latter, shipwreck is sure. No one can absolutely prevent him from choosing the wrong course, for there is no compulsion to make a man good unless he desires it in his own heart. When one recognizes that he is steering his own ship and has control of his destiny, the sense of personal responsibility seizes upon his mind, and no longer can he drift about, the sport of every breeze of the passions. He is the connecting ray and has learned that he must become a part of the God within himself, for in no other manner can he hope to avoid the dangerous shoals and hidden rocks surrounding him on his life journey.

The "Fall of Man" related in the Bible, in one aspect allegorizes the entrance of the connecting ray into humanity. "Falls" occur continually in all kingdoms. They represent the descent of the higher "lives" or entities from a more advanced kingdom to a lower, that by embodying themselves in the lower the latter may be imbued with the essence of the higher, and made to progress. This is an important factor in evolution, for as Drummond says, "No entity can raise itself to a higher condition, but requires help from above." The soul "fell" by connecting itself with the four lower principles, incarnating in mindless man by giving him its reflection, the faculty of reason. By the fall,

Adam ate of the fruit of the "tree of the knowledge of good and evil." At this juncture, Adam obtained a mind, the power to compare and contrast opposites, such as good and evil, pleasure and pain. The triangle, the Christos, "fell" by connecting itself with Adam (the quaternary), giving to the animal a mind, the connecting ray. "As in Adam all die, so in Christ shall all be made alive."

This symbology is carried further by the serpent deceiving Eve. In ancient writings, the serpent stood for the divine soul; it is the "Serpent of Wisdom." When the soul first endows man with mind, the latter, not yet being under control, acts as a deceiver. The animal, under the impulse of instinct, satisfies hunger, thirst and other bodily appetites, and ceases when they are appeased. Man under the guidance of an uncontrolled mind allows the faculty of imagination to lead him on to gluttony, drunkenness and prostitution of bodily functions. Instead of ceasing when the natural appetite is appeased, he associates pleasure with eating and drinking, and gives way to selfish indulgences.

Whenever we permit selfish passions to dominate, the law of Karma brings retribution in the form of troubles and trials,—not to punish, but to teach us to control our desires. The will is strengthened if we forcibly lift ourselves out of difficulties and learn self-control, and will eventually endow us with the power to refuse to succumb, however subtle the temptations which assail us.

The One Life finds its highest material manifestation in humanity. The experience gained by the "lives" in lower kingdoms fits them to enter humanity, when the consciousness of the animal gradually merges into the self-consciousness of the human being.

Man's destiny in this world is to find perfection; the connecting ray must not be broken until this is attained. Aspiration to become like the divine soul, and the practice of unselfish actions, are the best means of arriving at this perfect harmony with the One Life.

QUESTIONS ON CHAPTER X.

1. Whence comes the connecting ray?
2. Describe what the connecting ray is, and its purpose.
3. How can we strengthen the connecting ray in ourselves?
4. How did evolution prepare for the reception of the connecting ray?
5. Will the connecting ray always be necessary?
6. Who supplied the connecting ray? Whence came They?
7. Illustrate the illumination of the mindless men.
8. Who are the Elder Brothers?
9. Describe the two aspects of the reincarnating Ego.
10. How can a person be intellectual and not spiritual?
11. How does free will in man affect the connecting ray? Describe the two courses open to man.

12. What is the meaning of the allegory of St. George and the Dragon?

13. Give the meaning of the "War in Heaven."

14. What two influences affect the connecting ray?

15. How can we summarize the history of a life?

16. In the waking state, where is our consciousness usually centred?

17. Where is the consciousness in the sleeping state?

18. Has man free will to act?

19. Is it limited?

20. What does the recognition of free will confer upon us?

21. What must be our aspiration?

22. Give the meaning of the "Fall of Man."

23. Are there "falls" in other kingdoms?

24. What do "falls" effect? Describe the process.

25. What did man obtain at the "Fall"?

26. What "fell"?

27. How does the mind act as the "Serpent of deceit"?

28. Does Karma punish? How does it teach us?

29. Describe the evolution from animal to perfected man.

30. What is man's destiny?

31. How is it to be attained?

CHAPTER XI.

UNIVERSAL BROTHERHOOD.

"Bear ye one another's burdens, and so fulfil the law of Christ."—*St. Paul.*

"The evolution of a highly destined society must be moral; it must run in the grooves of the celestial wheels. It must be catholic in aims. What is moral? .... Hear the definition which Kant gives of moral conduct: 'Act always so that the immediate motive of thy will may become a universal rule for all intelligent beings.'"—*Emerson.*

Study of the One Life and its constituent "lives" makes it clear that universal brotherhood is both a law and a fact in nature; for everything in this physical world exists by reason of the mutual helpfulness that all parts render to one another.

In the lower kingdoms, this coöperation is compulsory, for the moulding force from a higher kingdom impels the "lives" to render assistance. It is this coöperation which holds together the forms for a period, and then relaxes, allowing the "lives" to break up their prisons and seek progress in new directions. It governs also among human beings, but with this difference: that the individual is not compelled, but must voluntarily determine to work in accord with this natural law.

Brotherhood is both a law and a fact in nature, taught by every object, and cannot be ignored without dire consequences. All "lives" belong to one great brotherhood, as sparks of the One Life or as drops of the mighty ocean of life.

Their coöperation is exemplified throughout nature's workshops, whether we examine a mineral, plant or animal. This spirit of helpfulness has been personified in the God who is ever loving his children,—the beneficent providence assisting all things to reach a higher state.

The scientist recognizes this idea, terming it the "Great Cause," the basis of evolution, from which all progress proceeds. This spirit of helpfulness has long been worshipped as an attribute of a personal God, to whom prayers are offered as a means of procuring material assistance. But instead of asking God to help us gratuitously, we should endeavor by our actions to deserve the assistance, making our prayers take a practical form. We should coöperate with nature, becoming agents for the divine law to carry help to others; for the law is just and will compensate us with the exact measure of our deserts. Prayer is the exercise of will in asking or demanding that the beneficent forces of the One Life act on this plane. We have latent within us the faculties of imagination and will, which if developed sufficiently would give the power to remove mountains. "Whatsoever ye shall ask in My name that will I do";—"If ye shall ask anything in My name, I will do it."

Real prayer is in the nature of a command by those purified in thought and will. They have acquired the power by meditation and the abnegation of self.

The practice of universal brotherhood would be the realization of the highest condition of harmony and happiness on earth, for it would be the application of the divine law of compassion, the loftiest attribute of the Deity. Were its precepts realized in our surroundings, social, national and political, suffering would cease and discontent, strife and misery disappear. Sin can be summed up as the breach of the law of brotherhood, and suffering and misery are the penalties to readjust the sin and to teach us to avoid its repetition. If selfishness were suppressed and brotherly relations prevailed, happiness, peace and contentment would reign universally.

The progress of the "lives" depends upon help being freely given and received, for all are necessary to one another; and in a similar manner we help or hinder those around us by our course of living. Selfish actions affect all, directly or indirectly. A person commits a fraud upon a bank, and in consequence others are treated as criminals until identified as trustworthy; and the presence of a few dishonest people in our midst necessitates the imposition of general restrictions. Equally do honest and reliable persons imbue their surroundings with an atmosphere of peace and security which is helpful as an example to their neighbors and introduces freedom into our relations.

"The unit is subservient to the whole," is an abstract expression of brotherhood. Following this rule we see that individual ambitions and desires must be subservient to those of society. The city must recognize the superior authority of the state, and the state, although autonomous as to local concerns, that of the federal government. Equally must the interests of nations be subservient to those of humanity as a whole.

Although universal brotherhood is recognized by many as the ideal state, yet unfortunately in practice the opposite is often ignorantly striven for. One endeavors to oust his neighbor by excessive competition; cities consider their own affairs paramount, striving for them at the expense of others; nations contend ambitiously for self-aggrandizement, sometimes building men-of-war and massing armies for the purpose of seizing the property of other nations. All these take place without a thought being given to the terrible readjustment awaiting such breaches of nature's law.

Instead of brotherhood, the practice of selfishness mainly rules, and we need not wonder therefore that the penalty of suffering is so widely experienced in all quarters of the globe. Famines, earthquakes, wars and rumors of wars, murders, suicides, shipwrecks, and general unrest and anxiety are but some of the methods employed by nature to bring about a readjustment of the breaches of the law of brotherhood.

Only by working for the good of all and not for ourselves alone, can we secure the best results even for ourselves; for only thus do we work in harmony with the One Life of which we are a part.

It must not be forgotten that each person is a part of the race, and it is imperative that we include ourselves in arranging the duties and aims of life. Duty has been defined as "that which is due by us to humanity." Our duties are first to those immediately around us, the circle being enlarged as opportunity offers.

We cannot avoid working for ourselves; the difference between brotherhood and selfishness being that, in the one case, we work for ourselves as *included* in humanity, and in the other we work for ourselves as *separate* from humanity.

We are all bound together by invisible threads, so that the action of each affects others. This union is true even on the physical plane, although the latter seems to exhibit separateness; for the "lives" composing our bodies are constantly being interchanged. The skin, hair and tissues change so continually that in a few years every part of the body is renewed. The "lives" thus liberated pass to other people, carrying the impress we have given them. Their vibrations are set to base or virtuous living by the impressions of our thoughts and actions, and tend to elevate or degrade in accordance with these impressions. Vicious living contaminates the common air, but upright actions make virtue easier for all, because of the binding together even on this lowest plane.

More subtle and strong is the connection as we rise in the planes of being, for the vibrations which pass from one to another become more rapid. Thought travels more swiftly than light. Others are affected by our thoughts and desires as these vibrate along the invisible threads of the vast web stretching around the globe and binding together all mankind. The company of evil-minded people produces a tendency to think as they do, whereas the society of the pure and noble suggests elevating thoughts. If we cherish only lofty ideals and kindly feelings, our part of the human web is lifted, and while those nearest to us feel it the most, yet the impulse of the upward trend reaches to the uttermost limits. Harboring evil thoughts and unkind feelings, and living base lives, give a downward pull to the web which affects all, but especially those nearest to us.

Brotherhood is a fact in nature which may not be ignored without self injury, whether we are conscious of it or not, or whether we live in accordance with it or fail so to do. Laws of life are laws of harmony; they are their own avengers, bringing readjustment with exact justice, so that every avenging angel is a personified representative of this reaction and readjustment.

While brotherhood is a great truth, the illusion of separateness exists in the mind, leading many to seek what they ignorantly consider to be to their personal advantage, regardless of others' welfare; but such actions harm their performers as well as all humanity. In such case, man forgets his oneness in the great Life, the memory being clouded by materialistic surroundings, and he bases his motive for action upon this seeming separateness of personalities; yet in reality the One Life binds all together, for the permanent part of man is not the changing body but the inner soul, the spark of the great flame.

The crying need of the world is that all should recognize that they are indissolubly linked together, and that none can help or injure another without doing as much for himself. There should be a determined movement to act in accordance with Brotherhood and weld it into our institutions, social, national and political; not merely as a theory, but applying it as a practical remedy for suffering. Acceptance of the fact of brotherhood does not imply that perfection has been attained, but that continued effort should be made to bring about its achievement. Each person realizes by his own lapses from the right path how difficult is this attainment; but continued effort will win, for self-conquest and altruism are the aim of Universal Brotherhood.

The Song of Life is heard by those who can attune themselves to the harmony of the One Life, which may be awakened in every heart.

QUESTIONS ON CHAPTER XI.

1. Is Brotherhood a law and a fact in nature? Give reasons.

2. Describe the method and result of coöperation in the lower kingdoms.

3. How does coöperation among human beings differ from its practice in the lower kingdoms?

4. How does the popular conception of God coincide with that of Brotherhood?

5. What is real prayer?

6. Are selfish petitions answered? Give reasons.

7. How is the power to pray acquired?
8. Is the practice of human brotherhood in accord with divine law? Explain.
9. What would be the effect in the world if brotherhood were practised?
10. What is sin?
11. Show how helpfulness assists progress.
12. Give an abstract definition of brotherhood.
13. Is competition in accord with brotherhood?
14. What is the effect of breaking this law?
15. Illustrate by every-day events.
16. Explain how we can best help ourselves.
17. Define duty.
18. Why must we work for ourselves?
19. What is the difference between brotherhood and selfishness, as regards working for ourselves?
20. How are mankind bound together on the physical plane?
21. Describe the effect our bodily particles have on others.
22. What effect have our thoughts and desires upon others?
23. Explain how it is they affect others.
24. What is an avenging angel?
25. Why are people selfish?
26. What does a selfish person forget?
27. What is most needed in the world to-day?
28. How do we realize the difficulty of being brotherly?
29. What is the "Song of Life"?
30. How can it be heard?

CHAPTER XII.

THE BASIS OF MORALS.

"Ye are not bound! the soul of things is sweet,
  The heart of being is celestial rest;
Stronger than woe is will: that which was good
  Doth pass to better—best."—*Sir Edwin Arnold.*

" The Kingdom of Heaven is within you."—*Jesus.*

"Moral philosophy, morality, ethics, casuistry, natural law, mean all the same thing, namely, that science which teaches men their duty and the reasons of it."—*Paley.*

The moral or ethical law is summed up in the practice of brotherhood, or helpfulness toward all beings.

The previous lessons have traced the basis of morals step by step, showing that Nature herself provides the foundation for right conduct, and that we have but to follow the path pursued by Nature to become highly moral beings.

The moral law is not an arbitrary arrangement subject to the caprice of kings or priests, or changing from age to age; neither is it based upon special revelation by any being, but is implanted in the unchangeable foundations of nature, and can be clearly traced and discerned by all who will use their spiritual understanding.

Study of the world's religions shows that Krishna, Laotze, Zoroaster, Buddha, Jesus, Paul and other great prophets, promulgated the selfsame moral laws. Each of these Saviours revived in man a knowledge of the operations of the One

Life, which had been forgotten, leading him to the recognition of his spiritual nature, which alone brings the sense of duty. Some religious bodies have claimed that this knowledge was revealed only to their particular prophet or founder, and was unknown before such revelation; but the facts of history and of nature contradict such a petty conceit, for the moral law is founded upon the laws of nature, and is ever the same, and man's duty does not vary from age to age.

The foregoing chapters have pointed out Nature's methods of operation, and her laws. We began by dwelling upon the One Life, which is variously described as the great force or energy, the cause of evolution, the Deity, the soul of the world. It is the One, boundless, infinite, eternal spirit of the world, the source of the moral law, from which all things proceed and to which they periodically return. The One Life is divided into innumerable "lives," each a soul in itself, whose relations are governed by the law of brotherhood, or helpfulness one to another. The existence of all things, from the rock to man, is due to the operation of this law.

It is thus at the very heart of nature, in the coöperation of the "lives," that we discern the law of brotherhood. Upon this mutual helpfulness of the "lives" is founded the real basis of morals. The "lives" are the types from which all things proceed, and the "life" in man constitutes the soul, his immortal permanent principle.

Next we studied "growth," which is from within outward. All "lives" proceed from the One Life, gradually covering themselves with denser garments, finally becoming embodied in this world. In the realm of the One Life is perfect harmony; for nature displays every part assisting the others. Disharmony creeps in when the "lives" have left their spiritual condition and have assumed material forms. If man obeyed the innermost promptings of his soul, peace would rule in his mental and physical surroundings. The soul within each of us is ever trying to guide us by the moral law into the paths of brotherhood, but we fail to listen to its voice.

Following this, we dwelt upon "cyclic manifestation," the universal law of alternate activity and rest, showing that rocks, plants, animals and men have their origin in the One Life, but periodically assume visible garments in this world, and then disappear for a time, to reappear again in other forms for renewed activities. Human beings are subject to this law; they live in this world for a period, then discarding their bodies they rest awhile, but return here to other bodies. The analogy of nature thus proves the immortality of man's soul.

Intimately connected with Reincarnation is the "law of action," or Karma; that every action has its effect, and that nothing happens without a cause. This law accounts for the great discrepancies in the conditions into which people are born. By coupling Karma with Reincarnation, we perceive absolute justice working along from life to life, bringing to each the exact deserts, good or bad, of former lives. We create our own conditions from life to life, and not even death relieves us of the results of actions, for they will return in future lives.

The basis of ethics is firmly established when the laws of Karma and Reincarnation are grasped, for man's responsibility becomes to him a patent fact. He will apprehend that absolute justice reigns—for nature knows no favoritism—and that all must reap what they have sown. If the law of the One Life be followed, harmony and peace will be our lot; but if we violate that law, injuring others by the practice of selfishness, rigid justice will bring suffering.

The following chapters dealt with incidental subjects; that "progress" is the rule of nature, the outer world existing as a schoolhouse for the "lives," which enter forms to gather experience and store it in their eternal essence. Thus progress continues perpetually by the accumulation of experience. This applies equally to man, whose storehouse is the immortal soul.

"Duality" was touched upon to explain the "pairs of opposites" in nature, arising from the operations of the mind, which compares and contrasts ideas and objects. Everything seems to us to possess dual attributes; but beneath is Unity, the object of our search. This duality shows life as separate from the plant and animal, the inner force distinct from its outer covering, and also the soul of man as separate from his body. The spiritual and physical natures of man are apt to be opposed to each other, but the moral law would lead us to control the lower, blending it with the spiritual, by obeying the law of the One Life.

The "sevenfold manifestation" in nature and man was treated, giving a close analysis of the seven planes of this world and the seven principles in man, and showing how man is connected with nature by these seven ties. We traced the spiritual and material, the permanent and temporary elements of man. The individual soul in each person, the Christos, that which is immortal and reincarnates from life to life, is part of the universal soul, or God, as the Son proceeds from the Father. The four temporary constituents of man, from the animal desires to the physical body, serve as a clothing or vehicle to enable the Christos to operate in this world, and to become by this association the Saviour of the "lives," raising them to its own divine state.

The "connecting ray" is the reasoning brain-mind, which forms the bridge between the Christos and its temporary vehicle. Progress depends upon our power to control the mind. The animal nature suggests the gratification of bodily desires, which leads to the attachment of the mind to sensual and selfish habits. The mind thus becomes the real battle-field, "for what a man thinketh, that he becomes." Efforts at self-reform must be backed by a sound philosophy from which the mind can find no escape. The basis of ethics or morals must indeed be immovable to convince us of the necessity of refraining from over-indulgence in those things which gratify and are pleasant to the animal nature ; for if the mind can find one small loophole for evasion, it will be readily seized.

Finally, we considered Universal Brotherhood as the practice of the highest ethics and morals. As the "lives" are parts of the One Life, mutually interdependent and necessary to one another, so are human beings inseparably connected. Forgetfulness of this great fact is the cause of strife and suffering in the world. If human beings learned the lesson of the One Life and the "lives," and, instead of competing to get the better of their neighbors, were to render help to those needing it, the harmony of the One Life would reign upon earth.

Study of the laws of Karma and Reincarnation convinces the unprejudiced mind that justice rules, and that the only way of escape from these present conditions is to apply the law of brotherhood to our associations ; for while man, misled by selfish ambition, vanity or greed, violates the great law of nature, there can be no other outcome than strife and misery.

To recapitulate the foregoing very concisely :

The One Life, the one creative force of nature, all-pervading and eternal, is divided into innumerable "lives." These are ever coöperating with one another, and by growth from within outward form the varied objects in this world.

The "lives," through cyclic manifestation, are constantly growing forms and casting them off, guided by the law of action. Thus they are re-embodied or reincarnated in mineral, vegetable, animal or human beings in exact accord with their own prior history. The purpose of these continued transformations is progress, and thus it is gained.

Everything has an inner, eternal part, and an outer, temporary covering, which form the "duality" in nature. The inner is divided for clearer comprehension into three aspects or principles, and the outer into four, making the seven fold manifestation. In man the reasoning mind is the connecting ray between his inner and outer principles, and forms the battle-field of his career, for he cannot progress permanently unless he voluntarily determine in his mind to follow the law of the One Life and the "lives," practising universal brotherhood or helpfulness toward all beings.

Ability in the individual to apply the moral law in daily life is man's most difficult attainment, but its acquirement is salvation in a true sense, for he is saved from the commission of sins whose result is suffering. Full application of the moral law involves being able to give up those things which the heart is set upon, whenever they become obstacles in working for the general welfare. This renunciation applies not only to bodily appetites, but to objects of ambition and vanity, and the seeking for place and power. It means the power to work for others at all times without any thought of how we may be affected. It requires a life devoted to helpfulness in deeds, words and thoughts, accompanied by an entire renunciation of self when the good of others is involved, not caring whether our actions meet with praise or blame.

Application of the moral law requires that we use the utmost energy and perseverance in the accomplishment of our duty to humanity; that we possess unswerving patience, and power to forgive persecutors and slanderers; that unbounded compassion and helpfulness be exercised toward all beings.

These lofty attainments of self-control and self-abnegation can only be reached by those who have learned that the spiritual nature is the real, that man is a soul. Enlightenment as to the One Life and the "lives," and the laws governing them, affords knowledge of the nature of the soul, the Christ within, as a living active principle, and gives faith in the existence within us of divine power and wisdom.

"Faith is the covenant or engagement between man's divine part and his lesser self." It is an enormous power, capable of bringing about this great change in man's nature, and enabling him to "remove mountains" of selfishness; but such faith must be founded on knowledge.

QUESTIONS ON CHAPTER XII.

1. How can the moral law be summed up?
2. What provides the foundation for right conduct?
3. Why cannot human beings change the basis of the moral law?

4. What was the mission of the world's Saviours?

5. In what respect are their teachings identical?

6. What leads to the performance of duty?

7. Why cannot any religious body rightfully claim to monopolize moral teachings?

8. What bearing on morals has the "One Life"?

9. What bearing on morals have the "lives"?

10. Where do we discover the basis of the moral law?

11. What bearing on morals has "Growth"?

12. What should man listen to and obey?

13. What bearing on morals has "Cyclic manifestation"?

14. How does the analogy of nature point to an immortal soul in man?

15. What bearing on morals has the "Law of action"?

16. Explain why acceptance of Karma and Reincarnation gives a firm basis for morals.

17. What bearing on morals has "Progress"?

18. How does man progress? Does he lose at death the experience of the last life?

19. What bearing on morals has "Duality"?

20. How does duality in man's nature cease?

21. What bearing on morals has the "Sevenfold manifestation"?

22. What is permanent and what impermanent in man?

23. Why should the objects of the spiritual man be paramount?

24. What bearing on morals has the "Connecting ray"?

25. Why is a sound philosophy essential?

26. What bearing on morals has "Universal brotherhood"?

27. What is the lesson of the One Life and the "lives"?

28. How can we obtain exemption from misery?

29. What is man's hardest task?

30. Explain the real meaning of "Salvation."

31. What is necessary for man to gain perfection?

32. Upon what must faith be founded?

33. Explain how we can reach the highest goal through faith.

"A healthy soul stands united with the just and the true, as the magnet arranges itself with the pole; so that he stands to all beholders like a transparent object betwixt them and the sun, and whoso journeys towards the sun, journeys towards that person. He is thus the medium of the highest influence to all who are not on the same level. Thus men of character are the conscience of the society to which they belong."

"The lesson is forcibly taught by these observations that our life might be much easier and simpler than we make it; that the world might be a happier place than it is; that there is no need of struggles, convulsions, and despairs, of the wringing of the hands and the gnashing of the teeth; that we miscreate our own evils. We interfere with the optimism of nature; for whenever we get this vantage-ground of the past, or of a wiser mind in the present, we are able to discern that we are begirt with laws which execute themselves."—*Emerson.*

"But stay, Disciple . . . yet one word. Canst thou destroy divine COMPASSION? Compassion is no attribute. It is the law of LAWS — Eternal Harmony, Alaya's SELF; a shoreless universal essence, the light of everlasting right, and fitness of all things, the law of Love Eternal."

"The more thou dost become at one with it, thy being melted in its BEING, the more thy soul unites with that which is, the more thou wilt become COMPASSION ABSOLUTE."—*Voice of the Silence.*

www.ingramcontent.com/pod-product-compliance
Lightning Source LLC
Chambersburg PA
CBHW020144170426
43199CB00010B/874